A THOUSAND WORDS

A Thousand Words

PORTRAITURE, STYLE, AND QUEER MODERNISM

JAIME HOVEY

THE OHIO STATE UNIVERSITY PRESS
COLUMBUS

Copyright © 2006 by The Ohio State University Press.

Library of Congress Cataloging-in-Publication Data

Hovey, Jaime.
A thousand words : portraiture, style, and queer modernism /
Jaime Hovey.
p. cm.
Includes bibliographical references and index.
ISBN 0–8142–1014–7 (cloth : alk. paper)–ISBN 0–8142–9095–7 (cd-
rom)
    1. English literature—20th century—History and criticism. 2.
Homosexuality and literature—English-speaking countries—History—
20th century. 3. Art and literature—English-speaking countries—History—20th century. 4. American literature—20th century—History and
criticism. 5. Modernism (Literature)—English-speaking countries. 6.
Description (Rhetoric)—History—20th century. 7. Oscar Wilde,
1854–1900—Influence. 8. Visual perception in literature. 9. Portraits in
literature. I. Title.

PR478.H65H68 2005
820.9'357—dc22
2005018872

Cover design by Jon Resh
Type set in Palatino

CONTENTS

LIST OF ILLUSTRATIONS

ACKNOWLEDGMENTS

I want to thank all the people who helped make this book possible. Judith Roof first encouraged me to pursue my interest in modernist portraiture and later served as a tireless reader and editor. This book is indebted to her boundless enthusiasm, intellectual playfulness, and strong belief in the necessity of a political and theoretical literary scholarship that circulates textual pleasures. Countless delightful conversations with Neville Hoad convinced me that Oscar Wilde's life and work not only helped engender queer modernism but also continues to inspire flagrancy. Candace Vogler pushed me to elaborate the Lacanian aspects of portraiture and self-consciousness, generously read drafts of early chapters, and was and is always eager to talk about ideas. Heather Lee Miller at The Ohio State University Press read this manuscript and liked it, and her interest made publication of this book a reality. Others who read bits of this in its various incarnations and offered feedback and encouragement along the way include Shari Benstock, Lauren Berlant, Harriet Davidson, Marianne DeKoven, Mary Dougherty, Cora Kaplan, Jane Marcus, Lisa Marcus, Peggy McCracken, Mary Beth Rose, and Domna Stanton. Their continued commitment to feminist criticism is a light in the darkness. Mark Canuel, Jamie Owen Daniel, and John D'Emilio offered support and encouragement in difficult times. I want especially to thank Melissa Bradshaw for her passionate feminism, unsparing criticism, and unwavering love and support. This book owes a lot to her sassy femme spirit, and to the spirit of my mother, Marilyn Reich Hovey, who did not live to see its publication, but whose appreciation for witty gay men, strong stylish women, literature, and parties lives on in all of us who loved her. This book is for her.

Pablo Picasso (1881–1973). Portrait of Gertrude Stein (1906). Oil on canvas. The Metropolitan Museum of Art, New York, NY. Bequest of Gertrude Stein, 1946. All rights reserved, The Metropolitan Museum of Art.

INTRODUCTION

Remarkable for its sexual themes—marriage, lesbianism, fetishism, male homoeroticism, masturbation, impotence, reproduction, birth control, free love, and gender inversion, to name but a few—early twentieth-century Anglo-U.S. literature demands its readers' devotion. Like lovers, these texts ask that readers let go of old habits and adopt new ones. Like lovers, these texts require a high degree of attentiveness, sensitivity to nuances of tone, a certain self-consciousness, the willingness to enjoy someone else's playfulness, and openness to new and daring ideas. These books invade and possess you; to resist them is to miss the point. Sometimes they talk dirty; many of them were banned for obscenity. They can be euphemistic, suggestive, discreet. An extraordinary number of them are portraits, concerned with portraiture, and—as the theme of portraiture suggests—interested in the sexual, gender, and racial aspects of character, personality, and personal identity. Yet it took most of the twentieth century for critical work to appear that explored their themes of gender and sexuality. The reasons for this are many, but they chiefly have to do with the complexity of modernist-era gender politics, the academic fashioning of literary "modernism" as a movement composed primarily of white heterosexual male writers, the identity-based forms that characterize most feminist and gay and lesbian literary criticism, and the sexual closet of artistic "impersonality" that still informs accounts of early twentieth-century aesthetics.

In her landmark book on expatriate women writers, artists, and publishers in Paris between 1900 and 1940, *Women of the Left Bank*, Shari Benstock points out: "The attempt to define and describe a literary movement as complex as Modernism exposes the divisions and differences among its practitioners even as it plasters over the cracks in the walls in an attempt to create a smooth façade."[1] Benstock goes on to argue that despite the role that gender often played in some of these

1

divisions, "the assumption that gender *alone* can explain differences in social behavior and literary practice of male and female Modernists requires rigorous inspection."[2] Benstock's feminist work of attribution and reclamation was part of the wave of feminist work in modernism that brought such writers as Virginia Woolf, H. D., Gertrude Stein, and Djuna Barnes, among others, back into the literary critical mainstream as individual figures, but *Women of the Left Bank* made a compelling case for the central role of women in modernist movements in a way that had not been done before. Other work in the "Gender of Modernism" (to cite Bonnie Kime Scott's important anthology) soon followed. Sandra Gilbert and Susan Gubar went so far as to argue: "the literary phenomenon ordinarily called 'modernism' is . . . a product of the sexual battle that we are describing here, as are the linguistic experiments usually attributed to the revolutionary poetics of the so-called avant-garde."[3] Gilbert and Gubar's essentializing analysis exemplified the ways in which gender criticism relied on identity in order to redress what Lisa Rado calls the "selective canonization"[4] in modernist studies of male authors at the expense of female ones. Because gender and sexuality were linked concerns for the many lesbian women who figured in this era, work on the sexuality of modernism followed this identity model, with individual bodies and their desires reflected in the aesthetics of "lesbian modernism," "sapphic modernism," or "Sapphistries."

Though work such as Peter Nicholls's *Modernisms* illustrates the tension between the critical project of accentuating a lack of aesthetic cohesion in the field, on the one hand, and the continued demand in scholarship and teaching that it somehow remain periodized and coherent, on the other, the sustained attention paid to women writers, lesbian writers, and gay male writers, including writers of color, in the 1980s and 1990s helped consolidate a much richer catalogue of experimental writing than had previously been available, and "modernism" eventually came to seem less homogenous and more diverse. Harlem Renaissance writing became (somewhat) desegregated from the rest of Anglo-U.S. literary experimentalism. Work on queer modernisms such as Deborah MacDowell's important critical essays on—and edition of— Nella Larsen's *Quicksand* and *Passing*, Marianne DeKoven's *Rich and Strange*, Eve Kosofsky Sedgwick's landmark *Epistemology of the Closet*, Joseph Boone's *Libidinal Currents*, Judith Roof's *A Lure of Knowledge*, and Colleen Lamos's *Deviant Modernism* extended the feminist project of reading race, gender, and sexuality in the texts of this era. These primary and secondary texts helped break down the exclusions that lent an artificial coherence to "modernism" at the price of its stylistic heterogeneity and particularly gendered, classed, racialized, and queer voices. However, when queer theorists such as Judith Butler and Judith Halberstam began to use modernist texts such as Larsen's *Passing* and Radclyffe Hall's *The Well of Loneliness* to theorize more generally about gender as performance and performative, they abstracted twentieth-century gender from the art and literature that helped formulate it. This approach gave us an art of sexuality reduced to individual performance and individual identity, or groups of individuals performing the repetitive gestures of coherent identity. The "art" of sexual and gender identity began to seem separate, for the most part, from its older and more dynamic context as a modernist textual concern constitutive of group identity and queer culture.

The problem with this gender trouble is that the individualizing of sexual desire is itself part of the cultural tendency to reduce homosexuality to an aspect of individuality and individual taste, and this in turn has long colluded with conservative theories of artistic sublimation—disseminated by many of the writers of the era themselves—that sought to escape personality and the personal. Because heterosexual desire enjoys the status of a universal human attribute, its yearnings have rarely been seen as too personal, whereas homosexuality was viewed by European and U.S. culture as an unusual and specific pathology for most of the twentieth century, what Eve Sedgwick calls "an issue of active importance primarily for a small, distinct, relatively fixed homosexual minority."[5] This partly explains the ascendancy in the decades after the Second World War of certain strains of modernist writing and modernist interpretation—Irving Babbit's hypermasculine aesthetics, Ezra Pound's vilification of Imagism's feminine and lesbian poetics,[6] T. S. Eliot's insistence on artistic impersonality—as official versions of modernism that helped marginalize the queerer modernisms of the effete Oscar Wilde, the lesbian Imagist Amy Lowell, the queer apologist Radclyffe Hall, and the sexually reticent Eliot himself.

This closeting of modernism's queerness that began with the canonization of some of its writers at the expense of most of its writers went hand in hand with contemporary and later critical rejection of modernism's feminine aspects. Homosexuality, lesbianism, femininity, effeminacy, and the personal served as linked terms defining a decadent perversity that a more virile, normal, and heterosexual "modernist" impersonality could position itself against. For a time a lot of modernist-era writing simply did not qualify as modernist at all, and most of the best and most intriguing literary voices of the era were particularized, dismissed as too popular, or relegated to other literary categories by mid-century literary critics. Oscar Wilde was a decadent; Langston Hughes mostly concerned with race; Mrs. Woolf (as Hugh Kenner calls her in *The Pound Era*)[7] female yet, thank goodness, married; Amy Lowell too democratic;[8] Radclyffe Hall middlebrow and sentimental. All of these writers were also gay, lesbian, or bisexual, and all of them either openly or suggestively explored the aesthetics of homoerotic desire.

The fear of effeminacy that stigmatized fin-de-siècle modernisms continued to shape critical work on the literature of the era a hundred years later. As recently as 1988, Hugh Kenner felt perfectly comfortable skewering female pulp novelist Marie Corelli, the popular Wilde imitator, as representative of her culture's intellectual and moral decay. In *A Sinking Island: The Modern English Writers*, double entendres suffice as argument: "Marie Corelli's way was the pornographer's: spin out, spin out, find empty emphatic words, but keep it up."[9] Kenner's leering, suggestive homophobia a few sentences later invites readers to chuckle with him at the indignity of Corelli's lesbianism: "She had her rewards, costly summers on Lac Leman and a friend from whom, like Gertrude Stein, she was never parted."[10]

Yet despite continuing efforts such as these to consolidate late nineteenth- and early twentieth-century writing as a rejection of the feminine, queer, and personal, the moderns themselves were hardly in agreement when it came to impersonality as a defining ideal of "modernist" aesthetics. Maude Ellmann has convincingly argued that T. S. Eliot's impersonality, as well as that of his contemporary Ezra Pound, was far more ambivalent than either they or many of their subsequent critics have allowed; Ellmann notes the slippage in Eliot's sense of personality, which ranges from the notion of soul, to the philosophical and psychological subject, to the first-person speaker.[11] Virginia Woolf, of course, had an interest in personality; hers is one of the most famous lines in modernism: "in or about December, 1910, human character changed."[12] But while this statement, and the essay on character and invention that it comes from, is often read as a manifesto of literary impersonality, Woolf elsewhere stresses her disagreement with such a notion. In "Personalities" she uses the example of Keats to mount a refusal of impersonality that depends—as does most of her work—on the reader recognizing Woolf's signature sarcasm, the trademark of her authorial personality: "how difficult it is to be certain that a sense of the physical presence of the writer, with all which that implies, is not colouring our judgment of his work. Yet the critics tell us that we should be impersonal when we write, and therefore impersonal when we read."[13]

Is it any coincidence that the notion of artistic impersonality, of a particular subject struggling to make itself universal, arises in the late Victorian and Edwardian eras as a rejection of romantic and impressionist effeminacy[14] at the same time that the term "homosexual" comes into being,[15] and at the same time, too, that Freud is developing his theory of sexual sublimation, using the figure of the homosexual painter Leonardo da Vinci to suggest the necessity of repressing or transforming unacceptable desires? Joseph Bristow argues that "effeminacy became the main stigma attached to male homosexuality in the eyes of English society"[16] in this era, largely due to the scandalous revelations of homosexual sodomy brought to light by the Wilde trials. In Oscar Wilde's *The Picture of Dorian Gray*, the artist Basil Hallward espouses the ideal of impersonality in a vain attempt to keep his homoerotic tendencies under wraps; his tragedy is that his best painting, the picture of Dorian Gray, is brilliant precisely because it is too personal, yet too full of his own desire for his young sitter, he fears, to be given the public viewing so fine a painting deserves.

This book argues that modern writing is obsessed with personality as well as impersonality, that "personality" and the personal often served as a euphemism for the sexual particularity of homoerotic desire, and that the (mostly) literary portrait—one of the more prominent forms of experimentalism in late nineteenth- and early twentieth-century writing—functioned as a dynamic aesthetic mechanism that formulated the homoerotic, the lesbian, and the perversely gendered as attributes of particular individual personalities and of communal, cultural group identities. The queerly modern experimental literature of this era uses the self-reflective dynamics of portraiture to invent queer moderns as sexually perverse subjects who circulate style, personality, self-invention, and impersonation as diversionary, playful elements that also undermine the moral and aesthetic rules of normal society and normal culture. The literary portraits of this era range from overtly fictional presentations of character, such as Oscar Wilde's *The Picture of Dorian Gray* or T. S. Eliot's "The Love-Song of J. Alfred Prufrock," to stylized renditions of recognizable real people, such as Compton Mackenzie's *Extraordinary Women* and Djuna Barnes's *Ladies Almanack*, to portraits of actual personages, such as Gertrude Stein's *The Autobiography of Alice B. Toklas* and Ernest Hemingway's *A Moveable Feast*. In these, writing is primarily enamored of its own self-consciousness, of the pleasures of looking at itself seeing itself, and is far less concerned with how it is seen, or judged, by conventional readers and critics.

A Thousand Words explores the ways in which these "modernist"

literary portraits enact this perverse, self-conscious, and stylish aesthetic. Instead of responding to the social demand, theorized by psychoanalysis as the fear of castration, that one take up normal gender
and sexuality under a watchful gaze, the "queer" characters and narrators in late nineteenth- and early twentieth-century literary, film, and
song portraits refuse to be normal, turning the look back on itself by
dramatizing it, distracting it, and soliciting it. To do this is to act perversely, write perversely, and read perversely. Even more extraordinary, however, is the insistence one finds in these portraits on dynamic,
group subjects. Because of the framing and narrative devices of literary
portraiture, desire, self-consciousness, artistic inventiveness, and
artistic and erotic appreciation circulate within and among a group
defined by its insistence that this affirmative circuit of desire is pleasurable. Self-consciousness in literary portraiture is an aesthetic
strategy, a dynamic and structural poetics that deploys sexuality as a
figure of a larger twisting of relationships—those between the viewer
and the viewed, the subject looking at himself, readers watching the
subject look at himself being looked at. "Modernism"'s modes of rendering the relations between the subjects and the look constitute a self-
conscious style that reproduces the self-consciousness of the characters
it describes. Indeed, self-consciousness and sexually perverse subjectivities are central to what we have come to recognize as the signature
innovations that characterize modernist styles.

   Unlike their less self-conscious Victorian precursors, modernist-era
portraitists emphasize the personas, imagoes, and personalities produced by perverse subjects to escape the rules of normal gender, sexuality, speech, looking, and social comportment more generally. In doing
this, these portraits perversely circulate the particularity, strangeness, or
unique "personality" produced by the art of portraiture as a quality
more indicative of style than it is a signifier of a person's true essence or
"real" nature. Personality style can thus be appreciated by performers,
audiences, spectators, and readers as an act of artistry and invention, an
aesthetic that is all about participation in a shared social world. Many of
these portraits are directly concerned with a variety of perversities,
including sexual and gender queerness, homosexuality, or lesbianism;
however, these emphasize personality as self-presentation, as a series of
aesthetic gestures that bring normative assumptions into question,
rather than as indicative of innate abnormality, pathology, or freakishness.

   These queerly modern portraits reveal different modernisms than
those laboriously constructed from more "high art" performances. First,

queer modern literary portraits capture the intersubjective dynamic of the look in painted portraits. This allows literary portraits to explore relations between narrators, subjects, readers, and style. The subjective crisis engendered by and presented in the fin-de-siècle and early twentieth-century scene of looking—a crisis that is both catalyzed and remedied by a kind of self-conscious self-invention—suggests that something about the look in modernity dislocates characters from their normal everyday subject positions and "forward-stretching" (to use D. H. Lawrence's term) narratives, producing instead subjects whose particular talent lies in the ability to solicit looking. At the same time, the surface style that enables these subjects to solicit the look is also capable of arresting the look when subjects take pleasure in their own performance, and then take added pleasure in the pleasure they are already taking. This self-amusement, consisting of a self-conscious pleasure that takes additional pleasure in self-consciousness, wards off scrutiny and censure by staging its self-sufficiency as a pose, a performance, and a pleasurable act of self-creation.

Second, queer modernist portraits focus on dynamic aspects of style and personality, presenting both the sitter's style and personality and the personality of the artist who renders her. The style of the sitter is the sense of herself, of the invented and elaborated personality she produces in response to the look, as she presents this self to the world. In the same way, the portrait as work of art relies not only on this personality produced by the sitter, but on the artist's interpretation of this personality, an interpretation that creates the particular style or signature of the artist's look. Thus we recognize a Sigmund Freud "portrait" or case study, a Stein portrait, a Modigliani portrait, a Barnes portrait, a Vanessa Bell portrait, by the style with which the artist or writer represents the dynamic interaction between the personalities of viewer, reader, artist, and sitter, a style produced to arrest the eye of the world that views it.

Third, psychoanalytic texts produced within this modernist zeitgeist understand this emphasis on style and personality as something produced by repressing or otherwise evading sexual difference and heterosexuality. In Freud's essay on the painter Leonardo da Vinci, *Leonardo da Vinci and a Memory of His Childhood*, the distinctive smile of the Mona Lisa, John the Baptist, and various other figures in Leonardo's portraits, such as the Virgin and St. Anne, marks the site of Leonardo's repressed heterosexuality. Style—the Leonardesque smile—marks Leonardo's refusal of normative sexuality. Working through Freud's insights, Jacques Lacan suggests that seeing works both ways. More specifically,

Lacan develops the notion of reflexive, self-conscious personality, of seeing yourself seeing yourself, to suggest personality as a stylized performance that represses the knowledge that one is also seen. This elaborated, stylized personality defends the subject and evades the Other's normative gaze through affectation, gesture, talking too much, satirizing others and one's self, and impersonation.

These three tendencies together produce a portrait of late nineteenth- and early twentieth-century "modernisms" as concerned with the refusals, resistances, and perverse aesthetics of a self-consciously queer art. This is not simply an effect of centering different texts as typical, but is also an effect of looking seriously, as this study does, at how queer modernisms render the aesthetics of looking at themselves. Considering the range of modernist portraits together, the odd texts of modernism such as the portraits of Gertrude Stein, Colette, Djuna Barnes, and Hemingway; other portraits or texts about portraiture considered outside of modernism, such as Wilde's *The Picture of Dorian Gray* or Nella Larsen's *Passing;* and the texts of high modernism usually read as character studies or dramatic monologues, such as Eliot's "The Love-Song of J. Alfred Prufrock," produces this alternate version of modernism, one more squarely concerned with subversive renderings of talking, reading, and desiring subjects.

Take, for example, this scene from Marcel Proust's *Swann's Way,* the 1913 novel that is the first installment of Proust's *Remembrance of Things Past.* Considered one of the masterpieces of European literary modernism because of its stream-of-consciousness technique and painstaking attention to sensual detail, *Remembrance of Things Past* chronicles the oedipal passions and voyeuristic impulses of its young narrator who in this scene watches through a window as a woman awaits her lesbian lover in a room as carefully arranged as a stage set, in which she assumes an attitude calculated to produce herself as she wishes to be seen. The most important feature of this production is the careful placement of her father's photograph on the table beside her:

> Presently she rose and came to the window, where she pretended to be trying to close the shutters and not succeeding.
>
> "Leave them open," said her friend. "I am hot."
>
> "But it's too tiresome! People will see us," Mlle Vinteuil answered.
>
> But then she must have guessed that her friend would think that she had uttered these words simply in order to provoke a reply in certain other words, which she did indeed wish to hear but, from discretion, would have preferred her friend to be the first to speak. And so her

face, which I could not see very clearly, must have assumed the expression which my grandmother had once found so delightful, when she hastily went on: "When I say 'see us' I mean, of course, see us reading. It's so dreadful to think that in every trivial little thing you do someone may be overlooking you."[17]

The boy watches unobserved as the two women kiss and chase each other around the room:

> At last Mlle Vinteuil collapsed exhausted on the sofa, with her friend on top of her. The latter now had her back turned to the little table on which the old music-master's portrait had been arranged. Mlle Vinteuil realised that her friend would not see it unless her attention were drawn to it, and so exclaimed, as if she herself had just noticed it for the first time: "Oh! There's my father's picture looking at us; I can't think who can have put it there; I'm sure I've told them a dozen times that it isn't the proper place for it."
>
> I remembered the words that M. Vinteuil had used to my parents in apologising for an obtrusive sheet of music. This photograph was evidently in regular use for ritual profanations, for the friend replied in words which were clearly a liturgical response: "Let him stay there. He can't bother us any longer." (177)

Mlle Vinteuil seems aware of her subjectivity as it takes shape in the field of vision, securing her lover's attentions by performing for the audience of the photograph, calling her lover's attention to her father's picture watching them, suggesting that others outside the window might be watching them together. Her stilted theatricality helps her invent herself as a creature who both expresses and reflects a style of being modern, a style characterized by its self-consciousness, its awareness of seeing itself seeing itself. She postures as a "bad" girl in order to appear naughty and modern to her girlfriend, but the narrator sees this as more proof of a virtuous nature than its opposite. By insisting on the public status of their lesbian caresses, both of these women construct themselves as modern, self-conscious, and perverse.

This self-consciously modern style helps Mlle Vinteuil and her lover diminish, parody, reformulate, and neutralize the censoring look of convention, here served by the stiffly bourgeois photograph of the father, whose gaze is framed, contained, and controlled in the seduction scenario. Looking at her looking at herself looking at herself, the narrator reads the desperation of a self struggling for a style:

> Far more than his photograph what she really desecrated, what she sub-
> ordinated to her pleasures though it remained between them and her
> and prevented her from any direct enjoyment of them, was the likeness
> between her face and his, his mother's blue eyes which he had handed
> down to her like a family jewel, those gestures of courtesy and kindness
> which interposed between her vice and herself a phraseology, a mental-
> ity which were not designed for vice and which prevented her from rec-
> ognizing it as something very different from the numberless little social
> duties and courtesies to which she must devote herself every day.
> (179–80)

The first thing Mlle Vinteuil's arrangement of her father's photograph
shows is how self-consciousness is necessary for erotic play. Mlle Vinteuil struggles for an individual style, one which will differentiate her
from her father, whom she resembles, and differentiate her gaze from
his. Resisting the father's gaze and playing to other gazes makes for
play, pleasure, display. At the same time that she resists it, however, she
needs the father's gaze to get things going, and to create herself as a subject who is read, seen, observed.

The presence of the young boy as voyeur (a presence libidinally
charged by the further layering of the adult voyeuristic narrator on the
persona of the remembering child) and Mlle Vinteuil's coy reference to
reading in the scene with the picture both serve to project the dynamic
web of desire mobilized by all these mirroring looks out into the world
and implicate readers in the narrator's voyeurism. "Reading" juxtaposes voyeurism and reading, visual and literary, and makes the photograph operate in a manner similar to the artistic visual conceit of the
portrait in Oscar Wilde's *The Picture of Dorian Gray*, which also parallels
the relationship of artist, subject, and spectator to that of author, characters, and readers. "Reading" as a euphemism for perverse sexual display suggests that the self-consciousness of reading—as dramatized by
Mlle Vinteuil's "reading"—fashions a mask, a playful self, a double, a
distraction to ward off the gaze, comprising some aspect of personal
style, character traits, or the "being seen-ness" defined through the
dynamics of the gaze.

Finally, however, and most importantly, reading framed here as
both performance and dynamic spectatorship gestures toward an ethics
of seeing, one that does not merely witness but identifies compassion-
ately with being seen as well as seeing, with the bravado of impersonation and self-fashioned personality as well as the abjection of resem-
blance. "And yet I have since reflected," the narrator muses, allowing all

the time between to enter the frame of the scene he remembers, "that if M. Vinteuil had been able to be present at this scene, he might still, in spite of everything, have continued to believe in his daughter's goodness of heart, and perhaps in so doing he would not have been altogether wrong" (178). Proust's framing of theatrical self-fashioning through this sympathetic identificatory eye intervenes in the terrifying field of the gaze, employing the diffuse polymorphous connectedness that desire makes possible in order to mobilize kindness, evoke pleasure and its loss, or pleasure as its loss, and allow language all its resonant play on the page. At the same time, this sympathetic social eye that remembers models reading for the reader—a reading that insists on the generative and generous possibilities of desire, of remembering, and of all the pleasures of self-fashioning.

This theatrical style, a sympathy with the necessity for the screen of posturing, appropriates the voyeuristic into the literary as the scene of posing, and thus the strategic personality of theatrical self-presentation becomes the rhythmic, posturing, performative language of modernist style. It suspends plot and character in its expert rhetorical display and stream-of-consciousness emotional and aesthetic digressions, delighting in its own deferrals. Watching, being watched, self-consciousness rises and takes wing, as if to say, "You want to watch? I'll give you something to watch." With this excess, and the way such display in literary portraiture foregrounds its medium of words, modernism becomes enamored with rendering itself seeing itself.

If Proust illustrates the dynamism of a sexual and gendered self-consciousness at the scene of portraiture, D. H. Lawrence interprets the scene of art as one of crisis, of modern self-consciousness as an erosion of colonial masculine self-confidence. In one memorable scene in *Women in Love*, a group of men lolling about naked after a wild party gather around a Pacific Island statue of a woman laboring in childbirth:

> They all drew near to look. Gerald looked at the group of men, the Russian golden and like a water-plant, Halliday tall and heavily, brokenly beautiful, Birkin very white and indefinite, not to be assigned, as he looked closely at the carven woman. Strangely elated, Gerald also lifted his eyes to the face of the wooden figure. And his heart contracted.
>
> He saw vividly with his spirit the grey, forward-stretching face of the savage woman, dark and tense, abstracted almost into meaninglessness by the weight of sensation beneath. He saw Minette in it. As in a dream, he knew her.
>
> "Why is it art?" Gerald asked, shocked, resentful.[18]

Gerald's question is crucial, for although he seems to be questioning the status of the primitive artifact in culture, he is actually challenging the artistic validity of representations of heterosexuality and reproduction. For Gerald, the gaze of the statue suggests a story he finds repulsive, a narrative that cycles through birth and death but always moves forward as her "forward-stretching face" looks forward. If her look is hetero-sexual and reproductive, his is queer, homoerotic, lingering on the time-less and the indefinite. The statue's gaze commences time, whereas Gerald's look stops time. Where the representation of a woman is to him all definition, all body and reproductive story, men's bodies are primi-tive and beautiful, like plants.

At the same time, these bodies are white and vague, in contrast to the racially other woman, whose body seems to mean to him one thing and one thing only. The prose of the text lingers in its own pleasant indefiniteness when Gerald looks at the men, a description of lovely and suggestive sounds that elude meaning. What exactly does Hall-iday's "heavily, brokenly beautiful" body look like? How can a man look "golden and like a water-plant," or "white and indefinite, not to be assigned"? Here the voice takes pleasure in its own circling narrative texture, conscious of itself. At the same time, unlike Proust's happily voyeuristic narrator, Gerald finds his self denied, his sensibilities unrep-resented, and his aesthetics overwhelmed. The demand of the statue's look castrates him when he agrees to take up a "normal" position around it rather than look at the men; the two meanings of "contracted" suggest his impotence at the very moment he agrees—contracts—to participate in the bargain of male conquest, Western appropriation, and heterosexual reproduction. It is significant that Gerald recoils from the scene of looking that the statue engenders, and that he does not see the statue with his eyes, which he reserves for the men, but with his spirit, which seems instinctively to recognize white masculine heterosexuality as a terrible machine that threatens to overtake his individual will.

Lawrence's text suggests the lingering aesthetic of Gerald's queer look, one where gazing at naked men results in words that have no meaning or referent outside of their own beauty, one whose pleasing sounds and startling images stop the flow of narrative and the trans-parency of description to offer the pleasure of language itself. Gerald's description of what he loves about Birkin could just as accurately sum-marize readers' response to Lawrence's writing: "It was the quick-changing warmth and vitality and brilliant warm utterance he loved in his friend. It was the rich play of words and quick interchange of feeling he enjoyed. The real content of the words he never considered: he himself knew better" (51). The backward look or the look that stops time also engenders a kind of pleasure in language, a pleasure that stops the forward roll of the story with an elaboration of style, a performance and a relishing of performance.

The most important result of this kind of reading, of this consideration of what it is these portraits are actually *doing*, is that the nonnormative project of modernist textual innovation is revealed as one sustained by many writers regardless of and apart from sexual identity or sexual content. This study extends three recent threads of work on literary modernisms: (1) the recent interest in issues of visual culture and modernism, as represented by Karen Jacobs in *The Mind's Eye*; (2) a tradition of studies of queer modernisms, such as Colleen Lamos's *Deviant Modernism* or Anne Herrmann's *Queering the Moderns*; and (3) psychoanalytic explorations of modernist preoccupations, such as Joseph Boone's *Libidinal Currents* and Judith Roof's *A Lure of Knowledge*. *A Thousand Words* turns from the more literal tracings of histories or identities to modernism's conceptions of itself and the way it renders those conceptions in the most symptomatic site: the portrait. This opens into an analysis of the ways self-consciousness and its inherent perversity are central to modernist innovation.

A Thousand Words explores facets of modernist self-consciousness by addressing four ways in which queer self-consciousness uses style to undermine normal and conventional expectations about the relationship of gender and sexuality to social behavior and artistic expression. The first chapter, "Picturing Yourself," reads Oscar Wilde's novel about a portrait, *The Picture of Dorian Gray*, and his short story on a similar theme, "The Portrait of Mr. W. H.," to explore how self-conscious self-observation—seeing one's self seeing one's self—perversely constitutes queer subjects as a group, rather than as particular and pathologized individuals. Just as the portrait of Dorian helps establish a series of circulating looks and circulating desires around the portrait, the artist, the sitter, and observers, so the framing trope of a portrait within a portrait reproduces Wilde's own loquacious theatricality, inviting audiences and spectators to share in the pleasures of queer looking.

Extending the self-consciousness of looking explored in the first chapter to a consciousness of talking, the second chapter, "Talking Pictures," explores how logorrhea, or too much talking, helps create exuberant and theatrical portraits. Focusing on how modernist style emerges from the pleasure of characters hearing themselves talking, this chapter looks at the 1927 film *The Jazz Singer*, T. S. Eliot's poem "The Love Song of J. Alfred Prufrock," Langston Hughes's "Madam" poems, Cole Porter's song lyrics, and Radclyffe Hall's *The Well of Loneliness*. Talking too much—chattering, prattling—is linked to femininity and sexual deviance. Women chatter; gay men chatter. By insisting on the pleasure of talking, logorrheic modernism creates a community of not only talkers but also listeners who share the pleasure of talking and who talk back—to sexual normativity, social propriety, and economic injustice.

The third chapter, "Caricature Studies," considers the proliferation of queer satire—satiric portraits of lesbians and gay men—in the modernist period. Satire functions by exaggerating the split between seeing and being looked at, a split that emphasizes the normative and controlling look and, in psychoanalysis, functions as a limitation or circumscription that signifies castration. But satire also takes great pleasure in playing with this split, attenuating or compressing it for its comic effects, and thus, satire circulates and even parodies the controlling look it uses to make its critique. Satire that emphasizes this split without deconstructing it, such as Wyndham Lewis's *Apes of God* and Compton Mackenzie's *Extraordinary Women*, denies the ways in which satire is always implicated in its own critique and ultimately upholds a kind of normativity. By contrast, Djuna Barnes's *Ladies Almanack* and Virginia Woolf's *Orlando* take great pleasure in turning the satiric look back on both hetero- and homonormativity.

Chapter 4, "Forgery, or, Faking It," argues that the theme of faking sexual pleasure in portraits of lesbian modernism is linked to the pleasures, perversities, and evasions of faking identity. Faking it, as seen in Colette's *The Pure and the Impure*, Nella Larsen's *Passing*, and Gertrude Stein's *Autobiography of Alice B. Toklas*, circulates an enjoyment of invented particularities, peculiarities, and persons, and revels in how elaborated queer personas play with normative notions of fixed identity and individuality. The form and structure of this subversion of identity cannot be misunderstood to be individuality, as can be seen by Ernest Hemingway's defensive imitation of Stein's *Autobiography*—a defensiveness that shuts down the playfulness of faking it and causes the self he tries to buttress in his memoir to collapse. By revising his past and trying to fashion an irreproachable authentic younger self, one enmeshed in but better than and independent of the social community of artists and intellectuals who mentored him, he takes refuge in a static individuality that cannot exploit the pleasures of a shifting, interpersonal and impersonating modernism, and cannot enjoy particularity as a pose, an aesthetic, an impersonation freed from individualism.

■ ■ ■

In 1907 Alice B. Toklas came to Paris and met Gertrude Stein at a gathering of artists and intellectuals at Stein's house, 27 rue de Fleurus. At one point, as recollected by Stein in *The Autobiography of Alice B. Toklas,* the narrative persona "Alice" tells Pablo Picasso that she likes his portrait of Gertrude Stein and relates his surprising answer, one of the most oft-repeated anecdotes in modernism: "Yes, he said, everybody says that she does not look like it but that does not make any difference, she will, he said."[19] Picasso's remark—or Stein's rendering of Picasso's remark—reveals a keen sense of modernist aesthetics as rooted in spectatorship, in readers, in an aesthetic response to a work that fashions subjects in the movement between sitters and those who observe them, and in the way history will understand them, their personalities, and the dynamism of art itself. Today we see Picasso's portrait as a likeness of Stein, just as we read the young Marcel in *Swann's Way* as a likeness of Proust, or identify the characters in Djuna Barnes's *Ladies Almanack* as likenesses of the women of Natalie Barney's circle, or associate Hemingway with the narrator of *A Moveable Feast*. But self-conscious, self-inventive "modernism" is also the shimmer of character outlines that do not fit the template of the personalities upon which they are modeled, the movement between self and self-invention that modernist style marks and elaborates in its playful circularity, indirection, and perversity. The invented personas and personalities of modernism are perhaps its most public face, its enduring legacy that has somehow remained such an elusive part of its project. Through these self-invented imagoes, personas, characters, and personalities, the stifling conventions of sexual comportment and social norms, the castrating demands of the look, the overwhelming imperative to be conventional, are sent up and perverted, circulated as part of a playful costume party where individuality, normativity, social status, and social stigma are poses. Here it is possible for readers, regardless of how normal they aren't, to enjoy themselves immensely.

The youthful Dorian (Hurd Hatfield) contemplates his aging and mis-shapen portrait in the 1945 MGM film version of *The Picture of Dorian Gray*.

1

PICTURING YOURSELF:

PORTRAITS, SELF-CONSCIOUSNESS, AND MODERNIST STYLE

IT IS THE SPECTATOR, AND NOT LIFE, THAT ART REALLY MIRRORS.
—OSCAR WILDE, PREFACE TO THE PICTURE OF DORIAN GRAY

Cleverly framed as a story about a portrait within a portrait, Oscar Wilde's 1890 *The Picture of Dorian Gray* is mainly concerned with how visual culture offers homosexual[1] men the possibility of a group identity. As the novel opens an artist, Basil Hallward, works on a "full-length portrait of a young man of extraordinary personal beauty" while the aesthete Lord Henry Wotton watches him. Both men are ostensibly admiring the painting that sits between them: "As the painter looked at the gracious and comely form he had so skillfully mirrored in his art, a smile of pleasure passed across his face, and seemed about to linger there. . . . 'It is your best work, Basil, the best thing you have ever done,' said Lord Henry, languidly."[2] The two men are interested not only in each other but also in the portrait's sitter, whose painted representation allows them to triangulate their desire, as well as the art that enables the expression of admiration and longing between men. Unfortunately, the circulation of these feelings is limited by conventional notions of artistic impersonality, as well as by the fear of social censure, both of which collapse the group dynamic of a visually expressed and expressive desire into an individual attribute. For Basil, such extraordinary individuality is risky:

> "Your rank and wealth, Harry; my brains, such as they are—my art, whatever it may be worth; Dorian Gray's good looks—we shall all suf-

17

fer for what the gods have given us, suffer terribly."

"Dorian Gray? Is that his name?" asked Lord Henry, walking across the studio towards Basil Hallward. (19)

Like the forged portrait that becomes the locus of literary and bio-graphical theorizing in Wilde's 1889 "The Portrait of Mr. W. H.," a short story about Shakespeare's boy-love Willie Hughes, the portrait in *The Picture of Dorian Gray* seems to be about a "real" person men use to organize their looking, their appreciation of masculine beauty, and their theories about desire and art. Not coincidentally, Dorian assumes a solid identity as the focus of their conversational attention at the exact moment that his likeness is assuming solidity under Basil's brush. This real and concrete person who seems to be the focus of both the painted picture and the novel who bears his name gives an individual form and figure to homoerotic desire, as well as to the larger circulations of desire and looking in both the room and in the novel.

In this classic example of what Eve Sedgwick has characterized as the epistemology of the closet, Lord Henry's homoerotic feelings are kept hidden by a determined unknowing, or at least, a pretense of guileless-ness. What is especially instructive about Lord Henry's unknowing here is the way it helps render homosexuality less threatening by reducing it from something that defines the erotic desires and practices of a group to a story about individuals, or a feature of individual characters. Thus Lord Henry's—and the narrator's—rapturous praise of Dorian's partic-ular beauty and personality helps the novel transform Basil's suspicion that they "all" are, as a group, extraordinary, talented, and attractive, and thus they "all" will be punished for being other than normal, into a story where only one of them—Dorian—is desired, and therefore only one of them will seem to be peculiar, extraordinary, and dangerous.

Homosexuality may describe the shared erotics of a social group as well as the sexual identity of various individuals, but it is more often used to particularize individuals. Wilde's *Dorian Gray* performs this col-lapse, and has in turn been viewed as a book with its own sexually and socially perverse "personality" ever since its author was stamped as one of the first publicly verified homosexuals in modern history in the 1895 trials that led to his imprisonment and notoriety. Indeed, the novel and Wilde himself have come to seem interchangeable, and like its author, the text has a particularized—if public—identity. It is a closeted text,[3] a per-verse text,[4] a camp text.[5] The novel is its homosexual subtext, a portrait—like Radclyffe Hall's 1928 *The Well of Loneliness*—of sexually perverse types, but one that, unlike Hall's sentimental manifesto, celebrates its own perverse aesthetics. For more than a century, homosexual male readers have turned its pages looking for an explanation of "their" sexual tastes, and for a way of being that combines aesthetic and moral resistance in order to refuse normative heterosexuality and respectability. Neil Bartlett writes of the aphorisms that open the novel: "The first method of interpretation is one of attack. For instance, I can find 'homosexuality' hidden in the most innocent or random of details, if my gaze is sufficiently obsessive or well-informed. All I need do is apply a characteristically gay skill—the gaze that catches the dropped hint, the note of excess."[6] In the novel, this "note" of excess is something Basil Hallward thinks he perceives in his portrait of Dorian: Basil thinks the portrait has "too much" of his feelings for Dorian in it, while Dorian later sees what he believes are his own excesses in the portrait's changes.

Modern readers who locate in the novel's pages the beginnings of modern gay sensibility have a sense of the subcultural work performed by its public circulation, its ability to solicit a perverse community of readers and bring them into being through its addresses, but readers also sense this movement in the novel where the social is reduced to mere individuality. Eve Sedgwick describes *Dorian Gray* as a novel that "condenses" its homoeroticism: "The novel takes a plot that is distinctively one of male-male desire, the competition between Basil Hallward and Lord Henry Wotton for Dorian Gray's love, and condenses it into the plot of the mysterious bond of figural likeness and figural expiation between Dorian Gray and his own portrait."[7] Moe Meyer similarly uses the language of "collapse" to interpret Dorian's murder of Basil as "a success that frees Basil from dependence upon the Other by literally enacting the collapse of subject and object."[8] This sense that many readers have of the novel's distillation of a circulating aestheticized desire into an individual life or figure can be found even in Wilde's best and most respected biographer, Richard Ellmann, who conflates art and life when he argues that Wilde's homosexuality determines the character of *The Picture of Dorian Gray*, and that the character of that novel, though not yet in existence, shapes the events in Wilde's life that precede it. Ellmann cannot resist reading Oscar's pivotal 1886 homosexual seduction of Robert Ross as one that prefigures—by four years—Dorian Gray's own lawless behavior in Wilde's novel: "For Wilde, homosexual love roused him from pasteboard conformity to the expression of latent desires. After 1886 he was able to think of himself as a criminal, moving guiltily among the innocent."[9]

As the long and continuing battle to declassify homosexuality as an illness suggests, normative culture has a stake in reducing homosexuality from a dynamic social desire among and between men to an individual taste, peccadillo, or pathology. As Jeffrey Weeks argues, disapproval of male sexuality in general and male homosexuality in particular continued to inform public attitudes in the late Victorian era, where social purity campaigns focused on the linked issues of prostitution and male homosexuality as personal, if gendered, excess, "as products of undifferentiated male desire."[10] Wilde's treatment of male-male desire in *The Picture of Dorian Gray* and "The Portrait of Mr. W. H." drew more negative attention to him than did his comportment, remarks, or behavior, emphasizing the perversity of looking—cruising, narcissism, voyeurism—but also, and most importantly, gesturing to this perversity as a shared social practice. Ellmann's language suggests Dorian Gray's outlaw anonymity, one where inner, "latent" desires isolate a man and make him lead a secret life, different from that of those around him—a life inspired, we are told, by the lonely, predatory life of Wilde himself. Yet Wilde hardly sought the individualized invisibility Ellmann's description suggests, and Ellmann himself concedes that while Wilde's marriage afforded him a certain measure of social respectability,[11] he did his best to undermine it with his writing. Unlike the dynamic likeness of Dorian Gray that is taken out of circulation by its sitter and hidden away in an attic room, the 1890 *Picture of Dorian Gray* and 1889 "Portrait of Mr. W. H."—both works with "too much" of their author in them—circulated publicly. Insisting on the presence of a public and communal perversity between and among the respectable male denizens of English life, Wilde could hardly be said to resemble the skulking, alienated individual criminal Ellmann imagines. Flaunting becomes a kind of hiding, while remaining a sort of flaunting— a resistant style not unlike the subcultural display Dick Hebdige terms "hiding in the light."[12]

Instead, as Wilde's writing and personal comportment shows, the conventional, socially normative reduction of "extraordinary" queer desire into a matter of individual taste and personal style, a reduction that neutralizes the social possibilities of homosexual community, is also resisted by the style that solicits looking with a vengeance, and emphasizes individuality to an extraordinary degree. This struggle to transform style-as-collapse into style-as-subversion is perhaps the foremost concern of *The Picture of Dorian Gray* and the reason for its emphasis on the dynamics of portraiture. Written by Wilde in part to demonstrate to his artistic nemesis James McNeil Whistler the superiority of writing to painting,[13] *Dorian Gray* uses the spectatorial mirroring of both the painting and the viewing of the painting to examine how being looked at and paid attention to produces the desire to be looked at, as well as to control the ways in which one is seen. The circuit of pleasure that looking sets in motion is suggested by the first scene in the novel and taken to another level by the novel itself, whose title—its main conceit— conflates painted portrait and literary portrait, producing the illusion of a portrait within a portrait. In Wilde's work, framing gestures such as portraits within portraits draw relations between portraits, self-reflexive perversity, and style. Someone who enjoys attention solicits the look by adopting a style that will fascinate. This style, in calling attention to itself, manages to invite and circulate the pleasures of looking and yet divert, distract, and parody the scarier aspects of the look, such as social scrutiny, judgment, and castration. The man who solicits attention cruises other men in the safety of like-minded friends and peers, per- versely keeping the look in the field of the same while inviting those in the know to join that field, that looking, and that pleasurable perversity.

However, as Basil's comments over Dorian Gray's portrait in *The Picture of Dorian Gray* certainly suggest, the threat of retribution by the gods for talent, beauty, and homosexual attraction and attractiveness menaces men with homoerotic tastes. At various moments, both Dorian and his friends experience a crisis when they feel themselves being watched, a crisis that psychoanalytic conversations would later liken to castration inasmuch as the look feels as if it contains the threat of pun- ishment. In Wilde's novel the protagonist, his friends, and even the nar- rator respond to this normative demand, the demand that one be ordi- nary in order to escape punishment, by turning the look back on itself, by dramatizing it, distracting it, or soliciting it. In doing this, which may involve the performance of an extraordinary individuality—making speeches, striking poses, adopting and discarding disguises, or making double entendres and shocking comparisons—characters behave per- versely, attracting attention to themselves only to mock both the atten- tion and the "self" at which such attention is ostensibly directed. This tension between the fear of sexual surveillance, on the one hand, and the flamboyant solicitation of the look, on the other, results in a literary por- traiture that is dynamic, perverse, and queerly modern, one that refuses the stigma of particularity by celebrating the group-constituting power of extraordinary individual "personality."

YOU'VE GOT THE LOOK

The specter of punishment that fuels Basil's anxiety about himself and his friends disappears when Lord Henry insists that their desire focus on Dorian Gray's portrait and then, as if by accidental extension, on

Dorian himself. Displacing the homoerotic desire that circulates between himself, Basil, and Dorian onto the portrait allows their erotic attraction to be manifested as mere aesthetic appreciation. However, Lord Henry also keeps that attraction moving, distracting his listeners with dramatic speeches where he airs subversively hedonistic views. Adopting the pose of peculiarity, affecting a character rather than seeming to speak sincerely, he is able to exhort Dorian—and the readers of the novel who listen to his speech along with Dorian—to live excessively: "Live! Live the wonderful life that is in you! Let nothing be lost upon you. Be always searching for new sensations" (31). Circulating his hedonistic views in the most theatrical manner possible, he constructs an audience, one delighted and distracted by the spectacle of extraordinary individuality he seems to embody.

The ways in which looking in *The Picture of Dorian Gray* constitutes a public invitation to shared perversity at the scene of the portrait is especially evident when Dorian sees his likeness for the first time. Here the public and shared nature of the look functions as a mechanism of sexual identification. Dorian looks at the painting from the vantage of another, as Lord Henry directs him to do. "'It is the finest portrait of modern times,'" Lord Henry congratulates Basil Hallward as the artist signs his name. Henry then invites the subject of the painting to see himself being seen: "'Mr. Gray, come over and look at yourself'" (32). Lord Henry treats the painting as a beautiful object that solicits the admiration of all three men in the room, tactfully ignoring Basil's earlier confession of the painting's autobiographical elements, and inviting Dorian to view his likeness as if it was his real self. In doing this, Henry uses the painting to organize the looking between men going on in the room. The men participate in Lord Henry's narcissistic invitation to "look at yourself," ostensibly admiring the painting instead of themselves and each other, though Dorian's doubled presence as both real-life person and representation makes Dorian—as well as those watching him look at his portrait—aware of the system of desiring gazes that produces first the portrait, then the occasion of its viewing, and then, finally, the group's consciousness of the viewing as a version of homosexual cruising.

Even the narrator's account of the scene emphasizes the pleasure of watching Dorian's pleasure in seeing himself:

> When he saw it he drew back, and his cheeks flushed for a moment with pleasure. A look of joy came into his eyes, as if he had recognized himself for the first time. He stood there motionless and in wonder, dimly

conscious that Hallward was speaking to him, but not catching the
meaning of his words. The sense of his own beauty came on him like a
revelation. (33)

Dorian's flushed cheeks and look of joy register not only his arousal but
also the arousal of those watching his arousal. Arousal works like that,
through looking at the arousal of others, as consumers of pornog-
raphy—like Wilde himself—knew. Not only does Dorian think he sees
himself being seen in his portrait, which captures the gaze of the artist
as an integral part of its rendition of him, but he is also ("dimly") aware
that Basil Hallward and Lord Henry are watching him awaken to the
beauty of the painting, as if it were an accurate likeness of how he is
regarded by others. Indeed, his sense of himself seems to come solely
from this encounter with this circuit of erotic looking, "as if he had recognized himself for the first time."

Yet everyone—especially Dorian—misrecognizes the relationship
of the painting to Dorian's own person. Rather than seeing how Basil's
vision creates a version of his person which acts as an eroticized image,
like a centerfold, between all three men, Dorian attributes his sudden
self-consciousness, his awareness of his own beauty and the beauty of
young men, to the painted likeness he believes holds the key to the mys-
teries of his personality. The text never says why this happens, though
the fact that it happens in response to the highly charged scene of three
men panting around a painting suggests Dorian shares Basil's discomfort with the free-floating quality of this circulating homoerotic admiration. Dorian collapses this admiration into a quality particular to his
own individual person, seeing the desire he sees in the painting as a representation of his own attractive fabulousness, and—later—using it to
justify his morbid self-obsession and self-loathing. He lets the painting
be a picture of his "real" self, rather than reading it as Basil's fantasy of
him painted in the presence of Lord Henry (which it is). He fails to see
how this desire is the product of a social dynamic, how it circulates and
ramifies between and among men, and how it needs to stay in that
world, both to feed itself and to inspire ever more beautiful feats of
artistic creation.

Basil Hallward, who thinks the painting is about him, comes closer
than Dorian to the "real" subject of the painting. Earlier in the novel, in
a conversation with Lord Henry, Basil condemns his "best work" as
somehow too personally revealing: "'An artist should create beautiful
things, but should put nothing of his life into them'" (24). Whatever the
painting reveals about Basil is far less important than the fact that the

painting organizes the desires of the men in the room around it, and yet Basil feels he has to deflect attention away from this. This is because the painting reveals the fascination men have for each other's beauty—a homoerotic fascination, if not an outright expression of homosexual longing, that Basil clearly shares with Lord Henry, yet takes great pains to insist is his, and his alone. Lord Henry claims to find Basil Hallward's work so fascinating that he demands to know everything about the beautiful boy whose likeness it is, while Basil, despite his friend's encouragement, insists that he will never show his painting publicly: "'I really can't exhibit it. I have put too much of myself into it'" (19).

Basil's ambivalence about the place of desire in the object of the painting, and Dorian's participation—however unconscious—in Basil's discomfort, sets up a larger ambivalence that structures the novel, an ambivalence about the subject-constituting function of homoerotic looking more generally. "It is the spectator, and not life, that art really mirrors," Wilde writes in the Preface to the novel. Basil's discomfort registers his consciousness of the demand by "the gods" that one be normal and ordinary. He personalizes and privatizes his discomfort, internalizing the scrutiny he fears, refusing to entertain the possibility that the painting might operate in a social field as something that might call out and circulate male homoeroticism in a way that cannot harm him. He rationalizes and perpetuates his culture's homosexual shame by reducing his homosexuality into something that is his only. Grasping the transformative impact of a dynamic homoerotic desire on both art itself and on his perception as an artist, he mistakenly reads the artistic results of his desire as nothing more than the effects of his own failed artistic sublimation.

Basil's position masks an elaborate defense of the closeted artist as a defense of artistic impersonality. On the one hand, he admits that his desire for Dorian has completely transformed his view of art, as well as his creative abilities: "'In some curious way—I wonder will you under- stand me?—his personality has suggested to me an entirely new manner in art, an entirely new mode of style" (23). In the next breath, however, he justifies the repression of his feelings by rejecting the per- sonal component of artistic expression: "We live in an age when men treat art as if it were meant to be a form of autobiography. We have lost the abstract sense of beauty. Some day I will show the world what it is, and for that reason the world shall never see my portrait of Dorian Gray'" (24). By insisting on sublimation and impersonality, that private desire—here equated with too much personality—has no place in art, he denies others the opportunity to be changed by his art and by the impulses behind it. He takes the homoerotic longing he invests in the painting out of circulation and thus takes the aesthetically transforma- tive aspects of those desires out of circulation as well. Ironically, his insistence on a more universal idealism actually particularizes the larger, more universal implications of his art. His equation of person- ality with the particular homosexual and impersonality with the absence of such feelings eliminates the possibility of a larger community that is not heterosexual.

THE SHADOW OF YOUR STYLE

Style, then, can address the crisis of homosexual surveillance by putting an individual, eccentric spin on group identity. As an interface between individual self-expression and subcultural social constitution, style becomes another vehicle where a dangerous homosociality can be reduced into a manifestation of the merely particular (and vice versa). The comportment of the dandified aesthete, of which Oscar Wilde— along with Whistler, Beardsley, and Beerbohm, most famously—serves as one of the best modern examples,[14] illustrates how individual style solicits attention in order to circulate the erotics of looking while sub- verting its normative demands. Wilde made his name in a culture that celebrated individuality by creating a buzz of publicity around his person before he became famous as a writer. "The attention he drew with his cello coat he was able to hold with his wit and enthusiasm,"[15] Richard Ellmann recounts of the astonishing coat Wilde wore to the Grosvenor Gallery opening in 1877 that changed colors when he moved. It is no coincidence that Wilde first expressed rhetorical style, theatrical manners, homosexuality, and artistic signature through his dandyism. The dandy's mode of theatrical self-presentation provided a semiotic model of style in visual culture that could be put to subversive ends, one that had successfully negotiated the divide between tradition and indi- vidual talent for hundreds of years. To be turned out in proper attire is to uphold the strictest kind of social convention; to be so well turned out as to become a kind of individual spectacle without drawing down reproach is one of the most extraordinary kinds of social and artistic bal- ancing acts.

Whether Wilde's "dandiacal send-up"[16] continued or subverted the tradition of the dandy matters less than his adoption of dandyism's emphasis on the self as spectacle, where style and visibility become a mark of value in a culture that itself values looking and being looked at above all things. Of Beau Brummell, the archetypal Regency dandy whose style of dress inspired the decadents and aesthetes a century later, Ellen Moers writes: "To the question—*What is a gentleman?*— which was to obsess poets and philosophers, novelists and divines, radicals and conservatives, the dandy made the most frivolous answer conceivable. He *was* a gentleman—it was a visible fact—by virtue of a 'certain something,' a 'je-ne-sais-quoi' which could not be defined—or denied" (original italics).[17] Brummell's courtly style both affirmed and undercut the aristocracy he seemed to emulate by emphasizing his individual transcendence of convention: "His arrogant superiority was an affirmation of the aristocratic principle, his way of life an exaltation of aristocratic society; but his terrible independence proclaimed a subversive disregard for the essentials of aristocracy" such as family and ancestry, class, national and social service, or money.[18] Rather than reducing particularizing behaviors, such as homosexuality, to individuality, dandyism theatricalizes individuality and individual taste, opening these out into the realm of public performance. Dandyism calls attention to the individual solicitation of the look, confounding public and private by making excessive individuality a public spectacle.

We see this solicitation of the look in the novel most obviously in the rhetoric, comportment, and individual style of Lord Henry, but *The Picture of Dorian Gray* also solicits the look in other ways, functioning as a portrait itself by exploring the relationship between the particularizing and social aspects of looking, as well as the particularizing and social aspects of an artistic "style" that also solicits and deflects various kinds of scrutiny. In this the portrait and its dynamics functions as something akin to the cotton-reel in psychoanalysis, as a subject-constituting object—or at least, as the object around which subject constitution takes place. Jacques Lacan recognized the importance of such an object to the "I" when, in revisiting Sigmund Freud's grandson's "fort-da" throwaway game with the cotton-reel, he surmised "that it is in the object to which the opposition is applied in act, the reel, that we must designate the subject."[19] Lacan's analysis of the relationship between the eye and the Gaze, the work for which he is perhaps best known, was a product of his historical moment—a moment where visual artists and writers were keenly interested in the relationship between desire and aesthetics, and where many of them incorporated desire into aesthetics by exploring the ways in which art operates as a site of circulating desires, looks, and personas.

Unlike the cotton-reel, however, a painting has several spectators, and thus its constitutive effects are not limited to one individual. The portrait's perceived ability to alternately destabilize and consolidate the subjectivities of its viewers in *Dorian Gray* anticipates Lacan's theory of the Gaze, formulated as part of his reconsideration of the modernist-era case studies of Sigmund Freud (which remain fascinating portraits in their own right), as well as his consideration of modernist literature itself.[20] One of the more important insights Lacan contributes in an effort to tease out the implications of Freud's observations about the effect of unconscious processes on the everyday life of individuals and cultures is the idea of consciousness as self-consciousness, as something that becomes possible only within the dynamic relationship of self and other. Lacan's theory of looking (gaze capitalized as Gaze), which gives an account of social relationships as a visual web of seeing and being seen, shows how the awareness of being looked at destabilizes the subject's sense of his position as unified and powerful. The look situated in space, while locating the subject as particular and personal by limiting the subject's perspective, also makes the subject aware of perspectives outside of his or her own body. These perspectives—what Lacan characterizes as the field of the Other—make the subject feel inadequate and fill her with the impossible-to-realize desire to be what the Other desires her to be.

Like Dorian Gray, Lacan's subject becomes aware of the Gaze from everywhere and attempts to escape its castrating and nullifying effects by appropriating it in a delusive attempt at self-empowerment. Lacan explains it thus: "The privilege of the subject seems to be established here from that bipolar reflexive relation by which, as soon as I perceive, my representations belong to me" (81). Avoiding inadequacy, the subject instead misrecognizes the Gaze when she imagines that she is the one doing the looking, that she is the one looking at herself being seen by others. For Lacan the split between seeing and being looked at is an important one to recognize, since it functions as a limitation or circumscription that signifies castration. This suggests that subjects who insist that they see themselves seeing themselves are using self-consciousness to refuse sexual difference, to ward off the look that demands sexual conformity, and to fashion alternative styles of self-presentation that resist and pervert normative forms of sexuality and gender.

The look that defines a person as someone who is seen comes from both inside and outside of them, splitting them into two different spectators: the one who seems to be doing all the looking, and the one who knows she can only see herself because she is seen from elsewhere. Lacan notes the tendency of subjects to repress the knowledge of this split by assuming that they are the authors of their own self-consciousness: "That in which the consciousness may turn back upon itself—grasp itself, like Valéry's Young Parque, *as seeing oneself seeing oneself*—represents mere sleight of hand," he notes in Seminar XI. "An avoidance of the function of the gaze is at work there" (74; original italics). Desire is not sparked by the Other, but by the self. Narcissistic self-desire, Lacan notes, is present in all kinds of love;[21] however, its degree of excess marks the difference between normal and perverse forms of sexuality.

Narcissism in psychoanalysis is an important site where homosexuality becomes legible as a collapse into the self, or into self-involvement. Here we see once again the repetition—or more likely the modern origin of the repetition—of the tendency to collapse homosexuality into individuality, into the individuated self epitomized by narcissistic self-absorption. Freud defines narcissism as "the attitude of a person who treats his own body in the same way as otherwise the body of a sexual object is treated; that is to say, he experiences sexual pleasure in gazing at, caressing and fondling his body, till complete gratification ensues upon these activities."[22] Freud immediately links narcissism to homosexuality as an "aberration" that is often found among aberrant types— a connection that allows narcissism to "claim a place in the regular sexual development of human beings." Like Lacan, Freud characterizes narcissism as a perversion in some cases, such as when it "has absorbed the whole sexual life of the subject," but as healthy in other instances, such as when it functions as "the libidinal complement to the egoism of the instinct of self-preservation." The queer aesthetics of narcissism have their roots in sexological and psychoanalytic constructions of both femininity and male homosexuality as narcissistic, constructions that, as Steven Bruhm points out, use narcissism and the figure of Narcissus to "stabilize a range of binarisms upon which gender in Western culture is founded."[23]

In contrast to this psychoanalytic version of homosexual narcissism, the self-conscious embrace of the strategic meta-narcissism of Wilde and the moderns solicits the look rather than refuses it, signifying the opposite of narcissism even as it performs it.[24] Seeing one's self seeing one's self in *The Picture of Dorian Gray* and "The Portrait of Mr. W. H." adopts narcissism as a strategic pose, one that both embraces a deviant position in relation to the gaze and dramatizes that position. Enjoying one's self enjoying self-consciousness aestheticizes, theatricalizes, and celebrates the excessiveness, queerness, and perversity that narcissism signifies. Unlike the private self-absorption of narcissism, the theatrical self-consciousness of *Dorian Gray* and "W. H." is a social invitation to perversity and participation in a shared aesthetic. Consciousness of one's consciousness in these works leads to exaggeration, the production of the self as a pose. Pleasure in posing, in theatrical self-production, allows Wilde's various characters and narrators the sense of being able to control how they are perceived. Self-consciousness deployed as a kind of personal style distracts, diverts, mocks, and resists the look—the Gaze—that is everywhere. It allows the safe reading of the queer man as peculiar and idiosyncratic by those who are not other to it, who share his idiosyncrasies, and who participate socially in the spectacle of his style by emulating it, serving as its audience, and appreciating it.

Lacan's subject's struggle to negotiate the consciousness of its own limits is signified through that subject's own styles of self-presentation. Style appears as a symptomatic response to the moment where the gaze becomes visible, throwing subjects into crisis by showing them how their sense of self depends so entirely on the look of the other. Lacan insists that one cannot actually elude the Gaze, though the effort to distract it can produce an extraordinary variety of masks, personalities, and doubles to deflect its scrutiny. In subjects undergoing extreme moments of self-dissolution, "in sexual union and in the struggle to the death," Lacan saw where "the being breaks up, in an extraordinary way, between its being and its semblance, between itself and the paper tiger it shows to the other" (107). This "paper tiger" of personal style Lacan found in the subject's moment of crisis performs two seemingly oppositional moves at once. At the same time style acknowledges the censuring and particularizing gaze, it dramatizes the attempt to ward it off, fashioning its resistance to sexual difference as an aesthetic gesture.

SMILE, PLEASE

One of the most striking things about the scene of sexual desire around the painting that awakens Dorian Gray to self-consciousness is that it is happening to a grown man rather than a boy, and thus suggests Dorian's sudden break with some kind of repression or sublimation, a repression or sublimation that requires amnesia. Dorian is supposed to be just entering his twenties, yet his naïveté suggests a child ten years younger. Like a child, Dorian lacks both self-consciousness and self-awareness. He lacks any notion, it seems, of his sexual appeal for other men, or his attraction to their attraction to him. This blankness is part of his appeal and marks him as guileless and sincere, but such complete ignorance seems a bit unbelievable in a man his age, even if that man is a product of late Victorian codes of silence and sexual respectability.

This blankness allows Dorian to enter the novel as an adult without a psychosexual history, an overgrown man-boy gifted, like a prince in one of the fairy tales of which Wilde was so fond, with magical powers of attraction and charm that the men who love him attribute to his remarkable "personality."

In *Dorian Gray*, "personality" is a euphemism for Dorian's homosexual attractiveness, an attractiveness that gets displaced onto the painting, one that calls out subjects as desiring and desired by setting in motion a cruisy, appraising, admiring, narcissistic gaze. Basil's desire is attributed to Dorian as an element of personality, the individual ability to fascinate others. This ability to incite desire extends to women as well as men, but seems to attract men primarily. Basil Hallward uses this idea of extraordinary individual personality to deny his own homoerotic attraction to Dorian by making attractiveness an attribute of Dorian himself: "I suddenly became conscious that someone was looking at me," he tells Lord Henry Wotton, recounting his first meeting with Dorian. "I turned half-way round, and saw Dorian Gray for the first time. When our eyes met, I felt that I was growing pale. A curious sensation of terror came over me. I knew that I had come face to face with some one whose mere personality was so fascinating that, if I allowed it to do so, it would absorb my whole nature, my whole soul, my very art itself" (21). Dorian's look calls Basil into an awareness of himself being looked at, and this awareness makes him conscious of his own look as well.

"Personality," then, is also a mechanism of displacement and sublimation. The notion of fascinating "mere personality" suggests the blank subject whose desires appear as his own but are really the projected desires of others, a function of the self-awareness of looking, being looked at, and being looked at looking. Dorian has no personality of his own at the beginning of the novel, where he impresses Lord Henry as a "gracious form" who might be "fashioned into a marvelous type," so malleable as to be "made a Titan or a toy" (40). Basil blames Dorian's gaze for his own homosexual attraction to Dorian, a gaze Basil evades by capturing it with his own on a canvas, turning the residue of his desire into art. Basil and Lord Henry displace their desire onto Dorian and reduce its social implications, but the insistence on the relationship of personality to the look also appropriates the look—Basil's, Lord Henry's, Dorian's—and makes cruisiness a function of art. This strategy of appropriating the look in *Dorian Gray* is important because it functions as the opposite of sublimation, the mechanism Freud and others used to define sexuality as the origin of aesthetics. In this theory, repressing sexual desire by transforming (sublimating) it leads to art. However, the intense presence of the look in Wilde's art insists that art can only take its power from untransubstantiated, unsublimated desire.

The concept of sexual sublimation arises in psychoanalysis in Wilde's era in order to help render opposite-sex sexual desire as socially productive and universal, characterizing homosexuality as an individual problem, one requiring disguise and transformation. While the concept of sublimation had existed from the eighteenth century, and was later taken up by moral philosophers such as Schopenhauer and Nietzsche in the nineteenth century,[25] Freud made it a central feature of his analysis of the drives and of civilized instincts, and it crops up over and over again in his theories linking the organization of sexuality to civilization and cultural achievement. Freud defines sublimation as the unconscious transformation of sexuality into other forms of creativity. In *Three Essays on the Theory of Sexuality*, Freud argues that sexual impulses are present in infants and children, but that a "progressive process of suppression" interrupts the development of these impulses, creating an "infantile amnesia" that "turns everyone's childhood into something like a prehistoric epoch and conceals from him the beginnings of his own sexual life."[26] At this point the child acquires the attitudes that will help suppress and redirect his sexual impulses, "mental forces which are later to impede the course of the sexual instinct and, like dams, restrict its flow—disgust, feelings of shame and the claims of aesthetic and moral ideals" (43). What concerns us here is that Freud's story begins with knowledge, knowledge that comes from the body through its sexual experience of the world, but that this knowledge is interrupted and suppressed at the same time that the child internalizes the aesthetic and moral ideals of its society. Freud is careful not to attribute cause to the effects he describes; in the story he tells, forgetting, repression, and moral consciousness all occur only in proximity to one another. However, in naming this process and arguing for its central role in the greatest achievements of every society, he makes what will become an extraordinarily influential claim about the relationship of sexuality to art: "Historians of civilization appear to be at one in assuming that powerful components are acquired for every kind of cultural achievement by this diversion of sexual instinctual forces from sexual aims and their direction to new ones—a process which deserves the name of 'sublimation'" (44). Sublimation here is a loss of self-consciousness, or repression of self-consciousness, that nevertheless seems to depend on self-consciousness in order to work. How does one know to redirect one's unacceptable desires into more acceptable channels?

Sublimation seems to require the kind of consciousness that erases its tracks after it has become something—or someone—else.

One of the most important modernist-era theories of sublimation—important because it directly links the concept of sublimation to both homosexuality and artistic endeavor—is Freud's 1910 essay *Leonardo da Vinci and a Memory of His Childhood*. Here Freud develops the theory of sublimation advanced in *Three Essays* through the example of the Renaissance master who seems to him to have "represented the cool repudiation of sexuality."[27] What is important for our purposes about Freud's theory of sublimation and Leonardo's work is Freud's notion of sublimation as something that leaves its mark on the artist's work, a process that operates as artistic signature and style as well as a point of libidinal transformation. Here sublimation's transformative disappearing act, where sexuality magically becomes art, is signified through a distinctly individual kind of stylistic marker—in this case, the Mona Lisa's smile.

Freud makes his case by beginning with the grown Leonardo, deducing that Leonardo's sublimated homosexuality masked a childhood attachment to his phallic mother. The impossibility of this libidinal attachment, combined with the absence of a father figure in his early childhood, results—Freud concludes—in Leonardo's "overpowerful instinct for research" combining with the "atrophy of his sexual life" in order to take the form of an "ideal [sublimated] homosexuality." This homosexuality expresses its energies through the pursuit of beauty and knowledge, a curiosity that manifests itself as "an intense desire to look," which Freud links to the child's longing for the mother's imagined penis. This exchange, repression, or sublimation is marked in the visual field of Leonardo's paintings as a smile that unsettles the spectator with its mysterious interiority and complacent self-sufficiency.

The Mona Lisa, conscious of being looked at, gazes back with a veiled, ambiguous expression, an insolent and dreamy smile that taunts spectators with what they cannot know about her inner thoughts and desires. Her smile teases viewers with the paradoxical nature of human sexuality, discrepancies Freud attributes to "the contrasts which dominate the erotic life of women" (58), but which are clearly contrasting cultural stereotypes *about* women. In these, women symbolize ambivalent attitudes about sexuality present in the culture itself, "the contrast between reserve and seduction," Freud writes, "and between the most devoted tenderness and a sensuality that is ruthlessly demanding—consuming men as if they were alien beings" (58). Note that his characterization of women as embodiments of sexual menace helps Freud make his case that the Mona Lisa's smile marks, in the same place, Leonardo's originary heterosexual attraction to his mother *and* his homosexual disavowal of that attraction. The menace of femininity, the mystery of gender and sexuality, and the veiled, even repressed, relationship of those qualities and drives to creation, reproduction, love, and art—all these are both buried and signaled in the smile that would become Leonardo's stylistic signature expression. From this disavowal, Freud argues, comes Leonardo's passion for art and science. Heterosexuality, homosexuality, all of culture's ambivalence about sexuality and sexual difference, and the origins of art and science as the highest achievements of culture, all are signified together in the mystery of a smile painted on a woman's face.

But the smile of the Mona Lisa is a self-conscious smile that nevertheless, for Freud, represents the paradoxical loss of self-consciousness on the part of the artist: Leonardo's forgotten disavowal of heterosexuality and transformation of homosexual impulses into art. The smile of La Giaconda, which is to say the style of Leonardo, signifies for Freud what has been lost to Leonardo, marking a point of sexual ambivalence and sexual disavowal signified in the visual field of the portrait. Freud concludes that "Leonardo was fascinated by Mona Lisa's smile for the reason that it awoke something in him which had for long lain dormant in his mind—probably an old memory" (60). Although this smile belongs to an individual immortalized in a painting, Freud notes that this smile comes to be associated with Leonardo's art and personality; "it has become a mark of his style and the name 'Leonardesque' has been chosen for it" (57). It is a mark of his style and its product, a distillation and a signifier of the sexual past he has forgotten. It is self-consciousness and the repression of self-awareness. Her smile represents her personality in the portrait of her known as the Mona Lisa, but that smile appears again on the face of Leonardo's John the Baptist, and in both women's faces in the Madonna and Child with St. Anne, the painting that alerted Freud to the meaning for Leonardo of Mona Lisa's smile, and which he analyzed as containing "the synthesis of the history of his childhood" (62).

Freud is able to make the connection between the smile and Leonardo's polymorphous infancy because of the dynamic relationship the smile sets in motion between artist, subject, viewer, and painting. The style of the smile captures the gaze of spectators and rivets them to the paradox of its public privateness, its self-conscious disavowal of consciousness, to the mystery it shows it is hiding, but one that is not hers alone, or particular to her. Mona Lisa's personality fascinates

Leonardo da Vinci (1452–1519). *St. John the Baptist.* Oil on wood. Many of Leonardo's figures display a mysterious smile similar to the one found on his Mona Lisa. Photo credit: Réunion des Musées Nationaux/Art Resource, NY: Louvre, Paris, France.

because that smile marks something at the threshold of memory and knowledge common to all who see it; Freud called it "indisputable" that "her smile exercised no less powerful a fascination on the artist than on all who have looked at it for the last four hundred years" (59). Here style—the mysterious Leonardesque smile—suggests a hidden interiority that exercises fascination on the viewers; at the same time, however, "style" is surface, signature, the hallmark of Leonardo himself, who uses it to solicit the Gaze and resist it. Finally, style—if we are to believe Freud—marks the site of sexual perversity and is created by that perversity as a kind of memorial or marker, in this case, Freud argues, for the heterosexual attraction to his mother Leonardo represses. Style, the smile of the Mona Lisa, is homosexual, gay, queer, and perverse. It displays itself even as it looks back, solicits, refuses, and remembers.

While Freud's reading of the smile as a dynamic signifier marking the secret to Leonardo's sexual past explains why it may have been significant to Leonardo, it also explains its fascination to others by suggesting that something about its mystery gestures to the lost maternal phallus that Freud equates with the playfulness and happiness of infancy. Writing of Leonardo's penchant for toys and mechanical inventions, Freud concludes that eventually this pleasure, too, likely gave way to sublimation and adult pursuits: "It is probable that Leonardo's play-instinct vanished in his maturer years, and that it too found its way into the activity of research which represented the latest and highest expansion of its personality." It is enough for Freud, perhaps, that this repression distilled into a smile remains as a mark of style, a product and indicator of the powerful psychosexual forces that go into the making of art. Yet even Freud is forced to cast a wistful glance backward, concluding his story not with a sense of the beneficial inevitability of sublimation and the repression of childhood sexuality, but with an air of melancholic sadness for the much wider world from which sublimation cuts us off forever. "But its long duration," he continues, "can teach us how slowly anyone tears himself from his childhood if in his childhood days he has enjoyed the highest erotic bliss, which is never again attained" (79).

STYLE, AND THE WORLD STYLES WITH YOU

Dorian's sexual awakening appears at first to be different from the one outlined in Freud's *Leonardo* essay, mostly because there is no narrator to insist, as Freud does, on the presence of the protagonist's forgotten childhood sexual history. Instead, Dorian's character is introduced by Wilde's narrator through conventions that resemble the "popular view of the sexual instinct" Freud describes at the beginning of his chapter in *Three Essays* on infantile sexuality, one "that is absent in childhood and only awakens in the period of life described as puberty" (39). To read Dorian's consciousness as one presented through this popular ideology of sexual development—that is, as a consciousness that believes it has no knowledge of the things it suddenly experiences—is also to see the ways in which the truth of this formulation is contested in the text, anticipating or perhaps even helping to formulate Freud's suspicion that sexuality precedes puberty. For nothing seems to account for the shattering impact of Dorian's sudden self-consciousness on his own personality, for his swift awakening to the visual dynamics of desire he apprehends in his portrait, and for his instantaneous apprenticeship to Lord Henry's brand of hedonist self-realization, so much as the existence of a prior self-knowledge Dorian has suppressed and forgotten. Dorian will spend the rest of his life trying to recover the lost bliss seductively invoked in the rhetoric of Lord Henry: "To realise one's nature perfectly—that is what each of us is here for. People are afraid of themselves, nowadays. . . . The only way to get rid of a temptation is to yield to it. Resist it, and your soul grows sick with longing for the things it has forbidden itself, with desire for what its monstrous laws have made monstrous and unlawful" (28–29).

Lord Henry's voice is the paint with which he models Dorian's likeness, and Dorian, sure that Henry is addressing him and none other, responds to the seduction of seeing himself being seen first with shock, then with pleasure. Almost immediately, however, he forgets that the words that have awakened him to self-consciousness are not his own. In Dorian's appropriation of Lord Henry's words lies his recognition of the desires he has repressed—desires, it is now apparent, that have a long history with him:

> For nearly ten minutes he stood there, motionless, with parted lips, and eyes strangely bright. He was dimly conscious that entirely fresh influences were at work within him. Yet they seemed to him to have come really from himself. The few words that Basil's friend had said to him— words spoken by chance, no doubt, and with wilful paradox in them— had touched some secret chord that had never been touched before, but that he felt was now vibrating to curious pulses. . . . Words! Mere words! How terrible they were! (29)

Dorian's incorporation of the narrator's outside gaze, corresponding to his reduction of the scene of desire into "mere words," allows him to aestheticize transgressive desires that are legally "unlawful," but it also allows him to both dismiss and emphasize the social world within which those desires are condemned. He mistakes Lord Henry's ideas, which also come from a world where dangerous books help circulate dangerous ideas, tastes, and identities, for his own, and thus fails to recognize the existence of a social world of like beings. Lord Henry's rhetoric both identifies and channels the sexual impulses Dorian has forgotten, but in doing so it also participates in the sublimation of those desires into words. Yet "mere words" marks a moment of recognition of the realness of artificial style for Dorian as well. There is nothing so real as artifice. With a sly wink to his readers, Wilde gestures to his own virtuosity, then, at the next moment, allows his protagonist to misunderstand the very insight that he seems to have been on the verge of apprehending. "Mere words" touch secrets that seem new, yet they clearly possess some kind of history, or they would not be secrets at all. "Mere words," and the voices that speak them, give precise articulation to hidden desires.

The production of style in the moment of self-conscious enjoyment in *Dorian Gray* suggests what psychoanalytic texts such as Freud's "Leonardo" essay also conclude: that is, that certain refusals produce style as a kind of supplement, residue, excess, and signature that marks the act of refusal. Leonardo's famous smile marks his refusal of heterosexuality, just as Lord Henry's rhetoric—and that of Wilde's narrators generally—marks the refusal of conventional morality. Dorian's smile marks his refusal to see himself as part of a group of men with like tastes, though the rhetorical performances that allow the narrator, or Lord Henry, or Dorian to snap their fingers at the self-important values of respectable society allow these characters to blend into each other as if they were the same character in the text, sometimes in the same moment: "Society, civilized society at least, is never very ready to believe anything to the detriment of those who are both rich and fascinating. It feels instinctively that manners are of more importance than morals, and, in its opinion, the highest respectability is of much less value than the possession of a good *chef*" (107).

The novel's narrative voice becomes a character in a play, one that enjoys itself enjoying itself as it says ever more daring and unconventional—if true—things. Having destabilized the normative sentiment that holds that morals should be valued above taste, the narrator goes on to celebrate artifice and insincerity as the true basis of social value: "Is insincerity such a terrible thing? I think not. It is merely a method by which we can multiply our personalities. Such, at any rate, was Dorian Gray's opinion" (107). If we understand style as a performance of individual virtuosity that both invites scrutiny and wards it off, then this

narrative voice embodies style. The narrator's transformation into a
stage character cites theatrical looking relations that depend on a notion
of style for their effectiveness, if by style we mean the affectations of
voice, gesture, and carriage that work with speech to help actors become
their character for audiences, and help audiences believe that well-
known actors are the characters they play. It is as if the narrator, like
Dorian himself (whose opinion, we recognize, is not his alone, despite
the text's insistence), is forgetting himself and trying on Lord Henry's
character. Doing this, the narrator undercuts his own reliability while
insisting on an "I" that is clearly not Lord Henry or Dorian: "Is insincerity such a terrible thing? I think not." The insincerity that allows
authors to make narrators, narrators to go in and out of the heads of
characters, and characters to "multiply . . . personalities" is the artifice
here of rhetorical style, which interrupts the plot with digression until it
is folded back into Dorian's character, allowing the story to proceed,
actually performing its own insincere proliferation of character before
giving way to the sincerity of a very moral plot.

We see this self-conscious style in Dorian's temperamental outburst
in response to Lord Henry's admiration of the painting, an outburst that
as it unfolds seems more and more aware of itself as a rhetorical and
dramatic performance in front of an audience: "'Oh, if it were only the
other way! If the picture could change, and I could be always what I am
now! Why did you paint it? It will mock me some day—mock me hor-
ribly!' The hot tears welled into his eyes; he tore his hand away, and,
flinging himself on the divan, he buried his face in the cushions, as
though he were praying" (34).

Watching his dramatic outburst, complete with tears, one is aware
that Dorian is watching himself being watched. He asks rhetorical questions, makes grand gestures, bursts into tears, and flings himself down.
This stylized, self-fashioned Dorian is the one Lord Henry sees as the
truest Dorian; Basil blames Lord Henry for corrupting Dorian, and Lord
Henry retorts: "'It is the real Dorian Gray—that is all'" (34). Henry's
response to Dorian's performance foregrounds the very issues of
authenticity and self-consciousness that portraits dramatize. Which is
"the real Dorian Gray"—the innocent Dorian Basil thinks he sees, and
renders in his portrait, the newly self-conscious Dorian who responds to
the portrait, and to his friends looking at the portrait, or the portrait
itself? For the last of these—and the seemingly most easily dismissed—
is precisely the one version the novel takes most seriously. As Dorian
remains ageless, his portrait grows ever more hideous, suggesting not
only that the dynamism of portraiture, its multiply-intersecting subjec-

tive visual and desiring fields, is its purpose and effect, but that it is precisely in the dynamism of the portrait where the truth of subjects
resides. The problem of this truth is that the slide between the individualizing and narcissistic aspects of personality and its theatrical imper-
atives—the slide Basil makes in characterizing the desires expressed in
his art as private and shameful rather than socially meaningful—is easy
to make in the context of a culture that equates beauty with both femininity and narcissism, and reads homosexuality as the product and
symptom of these.

Because his portrait ages and is punished for his sins while his body
remains young, Dorian's person comes to *really* embody the mask of
self-conscious personality that stands as a screen between him and the
censorious gaze of the world. The picture of Dorian Gray, on the other
hand, allows Dorian to move between the grandiose illusion that he has
escaped the gaze of the world, which would otherwise read the physical
toll of his excesses on his face and body, and the abject recognition that
his own gaze is part of a larger gaze he cannot elude, as he obsessively,
repetitively surveys the toll his life takes on his changing portrait. Even
the secret self requires an audience, if only to love it, and Dorian is no
exception, taking perverse pleasure in watching his sins being visited on
the portrait, much as the censuring gaze of the world might observe the
spectacle of retribution being visited upon his transgressive body: "On
his return he would sit in front of the picture, sometimes loathing it and
himself, but filled, at other times, with that pride of individualism that
is half the fascination of sin, and smiling with secret pleasure, at the mis-
shapen shadow that had to bear the burden that should have been his
own" (XX: 106).

Reading entails watching Dorian caught in the ambivalent web of
identification and disidentification with the image of himself he has
made, as he struggles to live up to the image of himself seen by others.
Just as personality is produced in the careless, brave affectation of his,
and Henry's, and the narrator's voice, reading is the consciousness of
self-consciousness that circles from the visual to the literary field, and
back, weaving the two together, insisting on the psychovisual components of reading as a vocabulary for and explanation of dynamic subjectivity in the visual world. The painting allows Dorian a unique
impersonality, the pleasures of impersonation where the posing and
posturing persona that wards off the judgment of the world takes on the
status of a true self. Dorian's mistake is to attempt a break with his past
by destroying the painting that signifies the self-consciousness he has
embraced, formed as part of the social dynamic of being looked at as

well as looking. And in the modern world, there is no self without this self-consciousness, and Dorian ceases to exist, except in art—in his portrait, and in the novel that bears his name *as* his portrait.

PICTURING LITERATURE

Written the year before *Dorian Gray* as a preliminary sketch of some of its major themes, Oscar Wilde's 1889 short story "The Portrait of Mr. W. H.," with its greater emphasis on intellectual improvisation and its heightened skepticism of the relevance of individual interiority, does what *Dorian Gray* cannot: imagine a world where the invention of personalities as part of a homoerotic libidinal economy can forge real social bonds between men. Like *Dorian Gray*, "Mr. W. H." uses the conceit of portraits and portraiture to explore how queer subjects come into being as part of a dynamic field of desire, though this story more obviously foregrounds discourse as its chief creative medium, and it uses a painted portrait to illustrate its theories celebrating discursive invention. "Mr. W. H." argues that talking, performing, and desiring other men all produce the kind of queer subject symbolized by the forged portrait of Willie Hughes, and by the literary "Portrait of Mr. W. H." of the story's title. The tragedy of the theory of Willie Hughes that the story explores, which is also the tragedy of the characters in the story who become seduced by the theory and by each other, is that all this talking, hypothesizing, theorizing, and performing never enjoys the status of historical truth. The "very thing that needs to be proved"—that is, the existence of a homoerotic intellectual dramatic tradition stretching back to Shakespeare and personified by the Mr. W. H. addressed in his sonnets—cannot be proven by reason, or passion, or intuition. Still, "W. H." succeeds as a "portrait" in its title and in its framed circulation of homoerotic desire in a way that the "picture" of *Dorian Gray* cannot, because "W. H." more fully participates in the dynamics of desire, invention, and looking that helps create queer subjects who recognize each other, subjects in process who generate homoerotic aesthetics, traditions, and culture out of their love of beautiful boys. For this reason it is useful to consider it, however briefly.

Forgery helps one realize one's personality in "The Portrait of Mr. W. H.," just as insincerity helps one multiply one's personalities in *The Picture of Dorian Gray*. "'You talk books away,'" a man named Erskine flatters Lord Henry in *The Picture of Dorian Gray*, "'why don't you write one?'" (44). This character also appears in "The Portrait of Mr. W. H." as the man who owns the forged portrait of Willie Hughes. Erskine first tells the narrator the theory of Shakespeare's boy-love, but he eventually dies in despair because he believes that the narrator does not believe in the theory or understand it. Erskine's presence as the skeptical narrator of an idealistic theory—a role later taken up by the narrator—makes his the voice that awakens the narrator to homoerotic intellectual desire, much as Lord Henry's voice awakens the young Dorian Gray. Like Lord Henry, Erskine helps convince the narrator that the "forging" of personality—the celebration of invention and performance over authenticity—is the best expression of both the pleasure of homoerotic bonds between men and the truest source of art.

As Erskine recounts to the narrator how a man named Cyril Graham once produced the portrait for him, he produces portraits within portraits: of friendship, of the characters in the friendship, and of the desire between them that gets transferred to a desire to discover the truth about Shakespeare's sexual and aesthetic passionate object. Meantime he unveils a painting for the narrator, watching his response to it as he tells his story:

> It was a full-length portrait of a young man in late sixteenth-century costume, standing by a table, with his right hand resting on an open book. He seemed about seventeen years of age, and was of quite extraordinary personal beauty, though evidently somewhat effeminate. Indeed, had it not been for the dress and the closely cropped hair, one would have said that the face, with its dreamy, wistful eyes and its delicate scarlet lips, was the face of a girl.[28]

The first story, then, is that of the effect of the painting, measured by the narrator/spectator's admiration of a boy who looks like a girl. The painting evokes desire, which in turn leads to theorizing, and to history. What is it exactly about the portrait that exerts its fascination on the narrator and on the readers of this story? At first, it is merely the boy's ephemeral and effeminate physical beauty. However, as its history unfolds, it begins to assert a deeper hold on the narrator's emotions. The form of the narrative becomes a series of frames, spiraling down toward the mystery at the center of the painting, the mystery of the existence of homosexual desire between Shakespeare and a boy actor, and the mystery of the desire on the part of all the narrators that such a boy exist, in order to prove something about their own existences they need desperately to know is true. "Mr. W. H." contains stories within stories, theories within theories, and personalities within personalities, framing complex interrelationships between men of different eras linked together by the compulsion to find, through personal intuition and emotion, literary scholarship, and deductive reasoning, the homoerotic object that inspired Shakespeare's sonnets to "Mr. W. H." For Erskine, who initially introduces the narrator to the portrait and theory, the theory and the portrait serve as an emotional link that binds men together, one that ties him to Graham, who originally formulated the theory, and stretches all the way back to Shakespeare. "He felt, as indeed I think we all must feel," Erskine tells the narrator, "that the Sonnets are addressed to an individual,—to a particular young man whose personality for some reason seems to have filled the soul of Shakespeare with terrible joy and no less terrible despair" (307).

However, what Erskine's search for Willie Hughes reveals to him is himself. The narrator, considering this story and then making it his own, makes Erskine's story his own as well: "A book of Sonnets," the narrator exclaims, "published nearly three hundred years ago, written by a dead hand and in honor of a dead youth, had suddenly explained to me the whole story of my soul's romance" (344). The past he really finds is not a material literary or historical past, but a felt, intuited, and imagined one whose repression is mirrored in the forgotten perversity of childhood, one that speaks to him precisely because he knows what he has forgotten. Putting himself in Shakespeare's place, he experiences the sonnets as a drama of living passions and living personalities, one that makes him conscious of his true self for the first time and changes him forever. "Strange, that we knew so little about ourselves," he marvels, "and that our most intimate personality was concealed from us! Were we to look in tombs for our real life, and in Art for the legend of our days?" (345).

The answer, of course, is yes, and the narrator concludes that "It was we who were unreal, and our conscious life was the least important part of our development. The soul, the secret soul, was the only reality" (344). In defining personality as "the secret soul," and self-consciousness as self-knowledge and the highest end of Art, the narrator seems to be advocating an extinction of the individual within a larger, more universal artistic tradition that therapeutically reveals the universal unconscious that all men share. Here the narrator is basing his conclusion on a new reading of Shakespeare, not the "tradition" that argues the sonnets were written to the Earl of Pembroke, or to Lord Southampton, to Shakespeare himself, or to "philosophical allegory." Instead, this new reading, a reading passed from friend to friend in passionate discussions that last throughout the night, stresses personality, particularity, and the type of queer temperament that sympathizes with the homo-erotic attraction between the playwright and the beautiful boy who dressed for the stage as a girl, a boy whose queerly effeminate grace, beauty, and voice caused men and women to fall madly in love with him, and rival theatrical companies to vie for his services. The person-ality of Willie Hughes that his "creator" Cyril Graham senses in the son-nets, whether real or invented, illuminates the personality of Shake-speare to him, and to readers like Cyril Graham and Erskine, causing them to recognize themselves as lovers of beautiful boys, moving them to acts of brilliant creation, despair, and suicide. On fire with what he has discovered about himself, the narrator writes a letter to Erskine, convinced of the theory at last.

Having done so, however, the narrator inexplicably loses all faith in the theory.

Why does the narrator lose interest in the theory as soon as he has expounded it most completely? "Had I touched upon some secret that my soul desired to conceal?" he wonders (345). Meanwhile, Erskine decides to sacrifice himself to prove the theory to the narrator just as Erskine's friend Cyril Graham once did to prove the theory to him. Erskine dies of consumption, and at the end of the story the narrator ponders the truth of the theory, ready to take Erskine's place and sacri-fice himself. In turn, readers of "The Portrait of Mr. W. H." take his place as enthusiast, scholar, and martyr, if only they become excited enough about the theory to recognize in their own "secret soul[s]" sympathy with Shakespeare's queer passion.

The story's title suggests both the forged painting, the hypothetical person sketched out in the theory by the narrator, and the larger frame of the story itself, encompassing all the other characters, theories, and narrators within its parameters. The author of the story must always die in order for the truth of Willie Hughes to exist as history, and in order to make room for the invention of other authors, and the revelation of other "secret soul[s]." Just as the narrator realizes that "the art of which Shakespeare talks is not the art of the Sonnets themselves" but "the art of the dramatist" (307), so he insists that "it is to the qualities inherent in each material, and special to it, that we owe the sensuous element in Art, and with it all that in Art is essentially artistic" (323). Emphasizing the framing and compositional aspects of portraiture, the personality of the artist and the gaze of the artist, as well as the subject of portraiture, the fascinating personality that looks back at readers, spectators, and the artist or writer, "The Portrait of Mr. W. H." emphasizes the reader as inventor, the inventor as critic, the critic as artist, the artist as reader, and so on in an endless and delightful interplay of the imagined and the social.

If Willie Hughes teaches us anything about the relationship of art and style to castration, sexual difference, sexual amnesia, and the recovery of lost or forgotten erotic energy, it is that authenticity has little bearing on what we know to be true. Having fashioned a literary portrait of Willie Hughes, sent off in the letter to Erskine, instead of a painted one, and thus committing a forgery similar to Cyril Graham's commissioned painting, the narrator realizes both the imperative and the inauthenticity of personality. "Whatever romance may have to say about the Willie Hughes theory," the narrator concludes, "reason is dead against it" (346). But this is precisely why the theory is valid. What Willie Hughes offers is a model for passionate creativity and thought that might come into existence in the field of desire, a model whose truth lies not in its historical accuracy but, like all art, in its ability to inspire. It is this that the narrator rejects, when, rejecting the theory, he also loses touch with what his heart had told him was real about himself, and claims to refuse to pass the theory on to the friends of his who admire the portrait. What he does pass on, of course, is the larger portrait of how homoerotic desire and the longing of subjects for a history and a culture create intellectual and aesthetic passion, and this in turn creates subjects and worlds for those subjects to inhabit. The "marriage of true minds" he imagines between Willie Hughes and Shakespeare, a marriage perpetuated between the readers of the sonnets and Shakespeare, and the readers of the sonnets and each other, goes on, immortalized in the short story whose title suggests a dynamic fascination between men as the source of an individually and socially generative queer aesthetics.

Jackie (Al Jolson) sings "Blue Skies" to his mother (Eugenie Besserer), their bodies oriented to face out toward the larger film audience, in the 1927 Warner Bros. film *The Jazz Singer*.

2

TALKING PICTURES

The early twentieth century was keenly interested in sound and the voice, as well as visual culture. This is true not only of poetry and prose, which the literary category of modernism characterized in this moment as experimental in tone, narration, and rhyming, but in film, which became increasingly preoccupied with recording technologies. Although several talking pictures of the era lay claim to the revolutionary status of the first sound movie, and critics have largely exploded the myth, perpetuated in later films such as the 1952 *Singin' in the Rain*, of sound as a sudden and cataclysmic industry event,[1] the 1927 Warner Brothers picture *The Jazz Singer* is generally regarded as the film that revolutionized sound. Although attempts had been made before to synchronize dialogue and music with film projection, *The Jazz Singer* made it big by featuring Al Jolson, one of the era's most popular vaudeville acts, as the protagonist of the film's title. Today *The Jazz Singer* seems remarkable for the way it places the voice at the center of the film as its subject and fetishized object. Throughout the movie, viewers are shown the protagonist singing, enjoying himself singing, and inviting audiences both inside the film and in the larger public to enjoy the spectacle of his enjoyment.

In one memorable and symbolically resonant scene, Jackie Rabinowitz—the jazz singer of the film's title—reunites with his mother for the first time since running away as a teenager, recreating his act for her, replete with frenetic stage patter and hammy, highly stylized crooning, in their little front parlor. The film is mostly silent, so Jackie's songs are situated in this silence as a huge pleasure for movie audiences, and this song is no exception. In the middle of the song, however, he stops singing to deliver a chatty monologue where he promises her the pleasures she has only dreamed of having:

Do you like that Mama? Well I'm glad of it. I'd rather please you than anybody I know of. Will you give me something? Shut your eyes. [He

47

kisses her.] And I'll give it back to you some day, you see if I don't. Mama darling, if I'm a success in this show, we're gonna move from here. Oh yes. We're gonna move up to the Bronx. A lot of nice green grass up there, and a whole lot of people you know. The Ginsbergs, and the Guttenbergs, and the Goldbergs, oh, a whole lotta Bergs, I don't know 'em all. And you know what else, Mama? I'm gonna buy you a nice black silk dress, Mama, you'll see. Mrs. Friedman, the butcher's wife, she'll be jealous of you, yes she will, you see if she isn't. And I'm gonna get you a nice pink dress that'll go with your brown eyes. Whad-dya mean no? Who's tellin' ya? Yes, you'll wear pink or else! Or else you'll wear pink! And darlin,' I'm gonna take you to Coney Island! And we'll ride the Shoot-the-shoot, and the Dark Mill. Ever been in the dark mill? Well, with me it's all right—I'll kiss you and hug you, you'll feel like it!

Film critics have remarked on the "manically gabby"[2] quality of Jolson's speech in this scene. His torrent of words creates the sensation of sound bursting into the movies, as if the silents—and the late Victorian and Edwardian culture of silent films—had repressed it. The notion of sound as the end of repression, holding back, or doing without, works on the larger level of *The Jazz Singer*, which uses both the voice and the look to offer audiences the fantasy of fulfillment beyond what their lives have afforded. The pleasure that Jackie's speech produces in his mother and in the film audiences watching her is equated in the film with the pleasure of sound, and the pleasure of sound in turn becomes associated with other kinds of pleasure: with looking, eating, wealth, travel, being seen, spirituality, sexual flirtation, and pre-oedipal happiness.

The previous chapter discussed Lacan's notion of "seeing one's self seeing one's self" as a late modernist rereading of Freud's work on nar-cissism, one that reads the pleasure of self-conscious pleasure as per-verse. More specifically, I argued that this pleasure is perverse because if the attempt to elude the gaze deflects the threat of castration, then it also signals a queer refusal of the normative gender and sexuality cas-tration is supposed to encourage and enforce. In this chapter, I want to explore the psychoanalytic suggestion that the Voice, like the Gaze, also organizes desire perversely in modernism's queer portraits, and that the self-conscious pose of staging one's self hearing one's self talking is analogous in many early twentieth-century texts to the insistence on "seeing one's self seeing one's self," a self-consciousness whose pleasure is organized along group lines rather than solipsistic ones. Like the self-conscious self-observation of seeing one's self seeing one's self, the emphasis in texts to staging one's self hearing one's self chatter can also be seen as a strategy that helps speakers refuse inscription in sexual difference; adopt a non-normative, deviant position in relation to the normative and castrating demands of the look; and invest objects with subject-constituting powers. Like the portrait in *The Picture of Dorian Gray*, which seems to be the likeness of a "real" person but which is really about all the people who together look at the sitter being looked at, songs and poems can seem to reflect something individual about "real" characters, but they can also emphasize the circulation of the pleasure of performance among multiple listeners, listeners who enjoy the enjoyment of the speaker. Indeed, the presence or imagined presence of an audience of spectators can actually create the effect of the performer "hearing" himself being heard—a pleasurable instance where self-consciousness produces the group that is its best audience.

As many modernist-era literary texts suggest, there is some connection between pleasure in talking and pleasure in looking, and an even greater pleasure to be had in taking this pleasure in looking and talking, staging it, and using its status as a performance to impersonate a character talking back. Such impersonation can be read as a joke, as someone "doing" an exaggerated version of themselves, but the pose struck in such impersonation emphasizes the agency and dignity of the performer. Staging one's self as a character in this way tacitly acknowledges what Susan Sontag termed "Being-as-Playing-a-Role."[3] A drag queen or a gay man camping it up makes it clear at any given moment that they are aware that they are a stereotype, but that they are going to self-consciously "do" the stereotype they embody nevertheless. Such self-consciousness can emphasize the performer's autonomy, his informed resistance to the notion of sincerity and personal essence, and his awareness of the difference between the respectable role he is supposed to occupy and the pleasurably queer one he chooses instead.

His chief rebellion, of course, is his circulation of this pleasure he takes in his own performance. The psychoanalytic system sketched out by Lacan insists that the voice and the gaze are two of the most important lost objects cut away from us by our socialization as gendered beings. Their loss is important insofar as it forces us to know ourselves through various separations, as separate from the others who see and talk to us. Even more important, however, is the way the Gaze and the Voice mobilize desire by reminding us of their loss to us in this separation, functioning as what Ellie Ragland calls "lure objects" that "never deliver the satisfaction implicit in them, but only titillate."[4] Kaja Silverman reminds us that when thinking about the function of sound in film, it is useful to remember Lacan's emphasis on "the discoursing voice as the agent of symbolic castration"[5] rather than as the sign of presence for which it is often mistaken in film theory. Slavoj Zizek argues that this voice terrifies us because it is disembodied and place-less, "a spectral voice which floats freely in a mysterious intermediate domain and thereby acquires the horrifying dimension of omnipresence and omnipotence, the voice of an invisible master."[6] A voice that owns its own pleasure might very well refuse this loss, this castration, this sexual difference, by insisting on its own sufficiency, or at least by staging this sufficiency as a circulating social alternative to the grim unpleasure of sexual difference.

In *The Jazz Singer,* Jackie provides pleasure with his voice, and he takes pleasure in providing pleasure as well. Like many a nonstop chat-terer, he clearly loves hearing himself talk. Jolson's highly stylized per-formance here both reflects and produces his self-consciousness; he clearly *knows* he is in a movie, and he conveys that he knows we know he knows. As such, he plays Jackie as a character who knows he is in a movie, creating the framed portrait of a person doing portraiture that circulates the look—and here, the voice—in a dynamic exchange between artists and audiences. His energetic hamminess resonates because he so clearly, so self-consciously enjoys producing it. He widens his eyes, raises his eyebrows, leers, and smiles even when his mother is looking down, playing to the larger gaze of the film's spectators even as he recreates the fiction of his stage show for her. The more he performs singing, the more he enjoys performing singing. Indeed, one of the most striking things about this scene is that the site of pleasurable apprecia-tion is Jackie rather than his mother; she is never more than sweetly, shyly encouraging, while he is all exuberance. His banter, too, is the-atrical rather than intimate, delivered to her in the form of stage patter during his own two-chord piano accompaniment, both of their bodies facing front, as if delivering lines to a seated audience. His pleasure in his own performance is the pleasure of the performance itself, and the film audience takes pleasure in him on his cue, rather than that of his "real" audience in the form of his mother. This kind of pleasure is the pleasure of the child, unshared and unsanctioned for the most part by the parents. More than his jazz singing, Jackie's modernity is signified by his pleasure in jazz singing, and in the pleasure he seems to take from having his pleasure watched, heard, and appreciated by others.

But this very modern pleasure is also a perverse pleasure. Talking in *The Jazz Singer* and elsewhere is often excessive, obsessive, fetishistic, self-absorbed, anxious. Like Jackie, modernist culture takes great plea-

sure in talking for its own sake. Michel Foucault has famously postu-
lated that the "putting into discourse of sex" has from the sixteenth century onward "been subjected to a mechanism of increasing incitement"
resulting in the "dissemination and implantation of polymorphous sexualities."[7] The 1902 definition of logorrhea that the *OED* gives is suggestive of both symptom and style: "Excessive volubility accompanying
some forms of mental illness; also *gen.*, an excessive flow of words, pro-
lixity." Psychoanalysis in this era constructs the talking cure as a kind of
logorrhea, or as talk having a logorrheic logic, in that its volubility is
produced as a symptom, or in search of it, or both. So, too, the literary
modernism that emerges in reaction to the middlebrow, sexually
respectable Victorian culture that precedes it is a stream of prattle, an
internal monologue that echoes everywhere, a virtuoso performance of
words upon words.

Michael North suggests that "linguistic imitation and racial masquerade" allow transatlantic modernist writers to "play at self-fashioning,"[8] pointing out that in *The Jazz Singer*, "Jazz means freedom to
Jackie Rabinowitz partly because it is fast and rhythmically unre-
strained but also because it is not ancestrally his."[9] North is dealing
specifically with dialect, rather than volubility, and draws a sharp contrast between the white writers it enables and the African American
poets who experience dialect as an insulting and enslaving appropriation. Unlike dialect, however, logorrheic modernism does not limit self-
fashioning and the pleasure of perversity to white writers. When
Langston Hughes's Madam in the "Madam" poems has a talking jag,
self-fashioning combines with a critique of racial, economic, gender, and
sexual oppression to bring Madam out on top as a woman of strength,
character, and humor. The obsessive racial stereotyping of Gertrude
Stein's gossipy narrator in "Melanctha"; the guilty yet defiant self-
reflexive verbosity of Molly Bloom in James Joyce's "Penelope" chapter
of *Ulysses*; the alcoholic rantings of Matthew O'Connor in Djuna
Barnes's *Nightwood*; the restless peregrinations of narrative attention in
Virginia Woolf's *Mrs. Dalloway*; the anxious, prattling self-ironies of
Prufrock in T. S. Eliot's "The Love-Song of J. Alfred Prufrock"; the exuberant and inventive showing-off of Cole Porter's song lyrics; the
campy riffs and queeny one-upmanship of Langston Hughes's Madam
in "Madam to You"—all are structured stylistically through the self-conscious pleasure of the talker enjoying hearing herself talk. Like Jackie
the jazz singer, who sings and jokes for both real and imagined audiences, logorrheic modernism watches itself talking, takes great pleasure
in its own performance, and suggests the perversity of this pleasure by

insisting that it circulate as the spectacle of its own pleasure, already framed for an audience constructed as an in-crowd of participants. The pleasure of the talker taking pleasure in herself, and the audience taking pleasure in this pleasure, is then circulated as the foremost pleasure of art.

Hearing one's self being heard, like seeing one's self seeing one's self, embraces self-consciousness as a strategy and pose. The subject does not merely fall for himself talking, like the narcissist falls for himself in the glass, but rather falls for himself being fallen for by others, and then falls for the entire spectacle. His ideal is not just his own image, or his own sound, but an aestheticized metanarcissism, the idea of himself falling for himself, his sound, his performance. This pleasure celebrates the critical distance between him and his image, or his vocal performance, while embracing the idea of the image, or song being sung, as a libidinal lure. This embrace of self-conscious narcissism as a pose attributes agency to self-consciousness.

The logic of this follows as something like: "Because I am conscious of my narcissism as a pose, I control it, and thus, I also believe I can control my being-looked-at-ness, as I myself control the way I look at myself. Similarly, if I enjoy my manipulation of that other lost object, the voice, so much so that my enjoyment of my voice becomes one of the effects of my voice that I also control, then I make the voice, rather than am being made by it, or rather, by its loss." This self-consciousness taken up as agency neutralizes castration by dramatizing its terms but rendering them harmless, traumatic to nobody. Instead, the trauma becomes a pleasure, an irony, a sarcastic read of the normal that twists it back on itself, making a shared pleasure out of this twisting and this perversity, a pleasure that invites its audience to share in it, a pleasure that creates a queer social world insofar as those who get the joke circulate this pleasure between them, as readers and audiences.

As I suggested in the previous chapter, one of the best and earliest examples of this style of perverse agency, of logorrhea as pleasurably self-conscious self-expression in modernism, appears in the spectacle of Lord Henry's talent for making pretty speeches in Wilde's *The Picture of Dorian Gray*. Returning for a moment to this extremely influential representation of a narrative voice framed as one enjoying himself enjoying his own talking, one sees the prototype of the modernist-era voice whose elaborations are part of the spectacle of self-consciousness *as* an artistic performance for its own sake: "The praise of folly, as he went on, soared into a philosophy, and Philosophy herself became young, and catching the mad music of Pleasure, wearing, one might fancy, her wine-stained robe and wreath of ivy, danced like a Bacchante over the hills of life, and mocked the slow Silenus for being sober" (43). Remember that like his author, Lord Henry responds to being looked at with talking, producing rhetorical style as a thing in itself, for its own sake. This artistry takes place in the field of desire that is also the field of vision: "He felt that the eyes of Dorian Gray were fixed on him" (43), the narrator informs us. His "extraordinary improvisation" (43) under the eyes of Dorian Gray is no less wonderful than the language of the narrator under the eyes of his readers, a narrator whose images of Lord Henry's speech appropriate that speech and transform it into rhetorical excess.

The link between the pleasure of this kind of logorrheic agency in *Dorian Gray* and its perverse refusal of the normative terms of castration can also be found later on in *The Jazz Singer*, when Jackie's father, whose presence as castrating father and religious cantor evokes both the Gaze and the Voice, stops the action and the sound of the film when he enters the room during Jackie's singing at the piano. Cantor Rabinowitz first interposes himself between Jackie and his mother by entering the room behind them in such a way that the perspective of the frame makes him appear to stand between them. Then, recognizing that Jackie is singing jazz songs to his adoring mother, he commands them both to "Stop!" The father's command insists that Jackie stop singing, to be sure, but most importantly, it insists that both Jackie and his mother need to stop their mutual pleasure, here rendered as a kind of infantile mother-son bond, in Jackie enjoying himself enjoying himself.

Jackie's pleasurable patter in this scene, which I quoted earlier at length, suggests how self-consciousness deployed as a mode of queer personal style functions as a gesture or series of gestures employed to distract, divert, and even mock the ubiquitous gaze. Oscar Wilde's writing sets up a template for how queer desire can circulate perversely, organized around the literal focal point of a portrait, or the metaphorical structure of literary portraiture. In Wilde's portraits, queer desire operates like narcissism in that seeing one's self seeing one's self organizes desire and looking in a self-reflexive circuit; however, his perverse portraiture differs from psychoanalytic accounts of narcissism in that it also requires the participation of an inside group of attuned gazers, or readers, who are constituted as a group subject by the circuit of looking that portraits seem to invite. In *The Jazz Singer*, jazz singing becomes Jackie's style, his perverse pleasure, and his non-normative identification, causing the rift between him and his father, as well as becoming an epithet his father uses against him: "you, you jazz singer!" Jackie's mother is his audience in the film, but Jackie turns his face more directly toward the live theater audiences when he sings, inviting them to share not only his mother's pleasure but also his pleasure in her pleasure, and in his own.

Moreover, while Jackie's decision to sing for secular audiences as a vaudeville performer rather than in the temple as a cantor like his forefathers is the ostensible cause of his exile from home, and Jackie's exile from home and triumphant return is the typical American success story, his expulsion also mirrors that of gay, lesbian, and transgender teenagers, as well as unwed pregnant daughters, when their libidinal pleasure conflicts with parental ideals of conventional heterosexual comportment. Jackie's pleasure in his voice is shameful to his father; Jackie's girlfriends in the film are fairly unconvincing romances; and Jackie even confesses to one of them that his career is more important to him than love. Jackie's libidinal bond with his mother and the vehemence of his father's intervention further strengthen the impression that he has chosen some other kind of pleasure than that of conventional heterosexuality. Finally, the shame surrounding Jackie's exile is marked by the removal of his boyhood portrait from the front parlor, a removal that his mother pretends was caused by the picture's fall, but which audiences know is a result of Jackie's fall into jazz singing.

The emergence of the voice, and of talking style, as an object of modernist aesthetics occurs at the very moment talking emerges as both symptom and cure in psychoanalysis, suggesting its status as both pleasure and containment of pleasure. As the origins of the talking cure in a fin-de-siècle psychoanalysis concerned with female hysteria suggest, the chattering personality who suffers from repression is understood as feminine, and talking acts as her sexual and intellectual outlet, marking her illness while serving as the cure. Talking also becomes synonymous with both femininity and feminization. Beginning with Breuer's patient "Anna O.," who named the relief she felt after confessing her symptoms her "talking cure," psychoanalysis came to rely on talking as a method for uncovering secrets, traumas, dreams, and fantasies.[10] Robert Graves and Alan Hodge saw the talking cure between the wars as one specifically aimed toward sexually thwarted women: "To be encouraged by a doctor," they write, "to talk about oneself in the most prattling detail, and to be listened to with serious interest, was a new and grand experience, especially for moneyed and lonely women who had had 'nervous breakdowns.'"[11] Their condescending dismissal of both psychoanalysis and the women who flocked to it records, however skeptically, how the exteriorized interiority of talking produces a kind of pleasure, in this case, a perverse pleasure linked to the expression of feminine emotional excess. Jackie's talking in *The Jazz Singer* feminizes him, as his bond with his mother feminizes him, but his exuberant style pushes back as well, taking up talking with a powerful gusto that makes it his. He occupies talk as he occupies blackface—as a performer performing self-consciously, reminding his audience at all times of the masks of style *as* style—as surface, persona, affectation, artifice. This self-consciousness gives form to his patter, a form that suggests intention and masculine agency even as his exuberant talk suggests the feminine formlessness of logorrhea. Jackie puts on chatter as he puts on blackface—to be modern, to be hybrid, to foreground style, to celebrate theatrical self-fashioning. Logorrhea allows him to be, in short, queerly modern.

DANDIES IN HIDING

Although *The Jazz Singer* made history in 1927, the patter of its main character was cultivated years before by Jolson on the vaudeville circuit. Indeed, the logorrheic voice whose self-deprecating patter has for nearly a century been seen as best characterizing the disaffected inertia of the moderns is that belonging to T. S. Eliot's Prufrock. "The Love-Song of J. Alfred Prufrock" was written just before the Great War, and there is perhaps no better example in modernism of how the pleasure of hearing yourself hearing yourself creates a particular style of ironic narcissism and thwarted masculinity than in the mournful chatter of this most despairing of dandies. The central character and speaker of the poem claims to fear the shallow insincerities of style, yet he stages his own absurdity, and the self-conscious enjoyment of his own voice, with disarming candor. "Let us go then, you and I," he begins, relishing redundancy. The "you" immediately stages an audience that stands for larger audiences, as Jackie's mother does in *The Jazz Singer*. This allows the speaker a theatricality, an awareness of himself talking to an audience, by staging that audience within the poem itself. His perception of other voices, especially those of women, threatens to overwhelm him, eliciting a stream of chatter from him as a kind of counterattack. We know from him, but only from him, that the city at dusk buzzes with the "muttering" of sexual discourse, of illicit encounters in "one-night cheap hotels," a discourse that speaks less of love than the end of love, like one lover badgering another in a quarrel in a "tedious argument / Of insidious intent." The speaker remains firmly in control, however, by insisting his voice be the one that distracts and redirects the looks and voices aimed at him with the self-parody of a childlike rhyme: "Oh, do not ask, 'What is it?' / Let us go and make our visit." Like Joan Riviere's masquerade of femininity, where the woman speaker makes self-deprecating jokes in order not to be judged by men as too masculine, the speaker in Prufrock affects self-irony in order not to seem to be trying too hard, or be judged as unmanly, unstylish, or dull. This archness characterizes the speaker's style in the poem, serving not as his personality, but as a mask of personality that deflects and manages the eyes and voices that scrutinize and interrogate him at every turn.

At the same time, the muttering voices and measuring eyes in the first few lines of the poem suggest the speaker's chatter, as well as irony, as a kind of compensation or defense produced in the conflict between an interiority where he feels safe and an exterior world of heterosexual demands. This is the kind of conflict produced by the scrutiny of being looked at and assaulted by voices, an assault Prufrock genders as female. The speaker's "room" is full of women talking: "In the room the women come and go / Talking of Michelangelo." The discourse of women concerning Michelangelo, as well as the idea of Michelangelo, provides a key to why the difference between inside and outside might produce so much Prufrockian talk. The notion of artistic sublimation that Michelangelo should represent, with its seamless transformation of unacceptable sexual impulses into artistic achievement and scientific inquiry, is resisted by the homosexual aesthetic of a Michelangeloesque sculptural style, replete with muscular nudes, that does not so much transform his homosexual impulses into art as serve to express and idealize homoerotic desire. The presence of such idealized male bodies, as well as the achievement such art represents, in this case only emphasizes the impotence and inconsequence of Prufrock's speaker, whose life is merely full of words: "works and days of hands / That lift and drop a question on your plate." Too taken up with "a hundred indecisions" to act or create, the speaker retreats into talking, style, and fashion as his forms of expression, "My morning coat, my collar mounting firmly to the chin, / My necktie rich and modest, but asserted by a simple pin." This feminine and effeminate art, however masculinized by understatement, only dooms him to further scrutiny: "[They will say: 'But how his arms and legs are thin!']." Prufrock's reverse dandyism, where he goes out into the world dressed as conservatively as possible in order to make a fashion statement that is not a fashion statement, can't help but draw an unfavorable comparison with Oscar Wilde, that greatest of dandies, dead just ten years when "Prufrock" was being written.[12] Any art the speaker undertakes, even dress, dooms him to an inadequate approximation of the style of great artists of the past, many if not most of whom seem to have been homosexual, and far surpass him in both genius and sex appeal.

The speaker's solution is to resort to the style of saying things, to speaking rather than comportment or bodily display. He finds refuge in the ability to ironically gloss his own descriptions, a disturbing habit that takes on ominous weight through repetition as the poem progresses. Faced with being scrutinized and dismissed by talking women, he talks back, launching his own stream of prattle. His talking becomes heroic because it is fated to fail, a futile effort that still speaks in spite of the certainty of this failure. From this countertalk in the face of the annihilation of his voice issues a subject defended by style from the talk of others:

> Would it have been worth while,
> After the sunsets and the dooryards and the sprinkled streets,
> After the novels, after the teacups, after the skirts that trail along the
>   floor—
> And this, and so much more?—
> It is impossible to say just what I mean! (99–104)

Note the rhetorical pleasure of repetition in the two "Afters," and the aesthetic daring of "sprinkled streets" in a sentence whose spoken quality is emphasized in the frustrated outburst of the last sentence. Despite the impossibility of communication, of being understood or understanding others, one can still say pretty things prettily. The "After . . . After" denotes a pleasure in oratory, and a consciousness of the effect of speaking, or sounding as if one is speaking. The attempt at poetry, even in its failure, is conscious of an audience, the "you" of "you and I" is presumably still listening. Nor does the impossibility of being understood preclude talking, or complaining: "I have heard the mermaids singing, each to each" the speaker mourns, "I do not think that they will sing to me." Instead of waiting not to be sung to, the voice appropriates the singing itself. Is it Prufrock, or the mermaids, or both, that speaks the lines "We have lingered in the chambers of the sea / By sea-girls wreathed with seaweed red and brown / Till human voices wake us, and we drown"(128–30)? For suddenly there is a "we," not a "you and I" between whom can be measured the ironic distance of self-consciousness, but a voice whose desire makes it ever more sure of its own incantatory power. In its siren song, the brio of this voice, its pleasure in itself, shows its hand. With a lilting rhythm like the movement of waves, the ironic, self-conscious voice of the speaker becomes one with the voices of the sapphic mermaids, who only sing "each to each" and prefer to "linger" around other "sea-girls." In this perverse and pleasurable moment, the moment Barthes views as necessary if the prattling text is to transcend its own frigidity "quite apart from bliss," readers become something more than mere address. The voice gives way to a queer interpenetration, relaxing the bounds of inside and outside. Without transparency, it says exactly what it means, but instead of foreclosing what it dares not hope for, it dares for once to desire something beautiful, and it lures us toward itself as the very fulfillment of that desire, that beauty.

TOPS AND BOTTOMS

Much of the queer humor found in the songs of Cole Porter resides in the arch relation of a speaker to traditional expressions of sentiment. While sometimes restrained to the point of pathos, as in "Begin the Beguine," Porter's lyrics are more often voluminous, chatty, and exuberant outpourings of American colloquial speech, replete with double entendres masked by an assumption of bright-eyed naïveté. Typical is this assertion of tongue-tied taciturnity from "You're the Top":

> At words poetic I'm so pathetic
> That I always have found it best
> Instead of getting 'em off my chest,
> To let 'em rest—unexpressed.

Despite this pose of incoherence, one that seems to emphasize the sincere value of real feeling over the more suspect sophistication implied by glib eloquence, what follows this prelude is one of Porter's campiest and most playful of songs, an exuberant invention fueled by the pure joy of combining unlikely sets of objects together by rhyming:

> You're the top! you're the Colosseum,
> You're the top! you're the Louvre Museum,
> You're the melody from a symphony by Strauss,
> You're a Bendel bonnet,
> A Shakespeare Sonnet,
> You're Mickey Mouse!

The invention of images uses its end-rhymes to reach even further: after insisting that "you" are not only the "Nile," the "Tow'r of Pisa," and even the famous "smile" on the "Mona Lisa," the speaker concludes: "I'm a worthless check, a total wreck, a flop! / But if baby I'm the bottom, / You're the top!"

What is exhilarating about this highwire display of ever-wilder idealization is its vast archive of superlative images, images that range from the strictest standards of artistic excellence—Shakespeare, the Mona Lisa—and architectural wonders—the Coliseum and the Louvre—to Mickey Mouse. The disparate associations get ever more random as the song progresses: "You're the National Gallery, you're Garbo's salary, you're cellophane!" is one breathless assertion. The jumble of high and low culture, of the extraordinarily varied but artistically and technologically wonderful elements of modern life all stitched together by the play of language, results in a song that enjoys its own efforts at tribute, its own ability to snatch rhyming objects from the vocabulary of everyday life and whirl them into a kind of juggling, off-the-cuff virtuoso performance of sheer inventive genius. The randomness of the objects assures the effect of spontaneity—these are too popular, too much a "man on the street"'s idea of nifty stuff, to be carefully thought out, weighed, taxonomized. Acquainted with the existence of "a rose," or "inferno's Dante," the speaker has no qualms about equating these with "the nose, on the great Durante"—an equivalence that only a person who did not really understand the importance of Dante could make.

Or is it? The pose of innocence, of gee whiz exuberance, allows the speaker to get away with the sarcasm of the conclusion "But if baby I'm the bottom, / You're the top!" Whether the speaker has really constituted the object of her admiration as the top can only be believed if one buys her guileless pose and reads her tribute as sincere. In the 1934 Broadway musical *Anything Goes* where this song appears, its caustic sarcasm is hard to miss. Indeed, the sly suggestion of sadomasochism that seems to be contained in these lines, of dominant and submissive sexual roles, is one any contemporary listener familiar with queer sexual culture finds hard to miss. While it is not at all clear whether "top" and "bottom" had any meaning for homosexuals in the 1930s that resembles the dominant/submissive associations one automatically makes now, "top" has for several centuries carried the sense of surpassing and besting a rival or opponent, at least according to the *OED*, and so it is not such a stretch to infer that "top" and "bottom" in Porter's time might suggest the sexual roles now familiar to queer and deviant sexual communities. Certainly an arch consciousness like Porter's would have appreciated the humor of simultaneously asserting the hypothetical necessity of the bottom—"But if baby I'm the bottom"—in order that the top position can exist.

In other words, even if "bottom" and "top" do not mean what we think they might mean, even if you do not know Porter was a homosexual, even if you are not familiar with *Anything Goes*, with its title song that ventriloquizes moral censure while exulting in moral decadence ("When every night / The set that's smart / Is intruding on nudist parties / In studios"), and which also featured the liminally gendered Ethel Merman belting tunes preoccupied with alcohol and cocaine, and even if you do not know other Cole Porter songs like "Love for Sale," the exuberant chattiness of "You're the Top" still evokes a queer aesthetic. It does this with its double entendres; its arch adoption of a guileless, normative heterosexual innocence around codes of sexual perversity; and its logorrhea, its sheer enjoyment of its own rhetorical virtuosity, its shameless rhymes, and its campy sarcasm, all of which combine to form a song that is all about the joy of style—its cleverness and wit, its invention, its outrageous juxtaposition of high and low culture, its self-conscious posing, its delight in its own performance of artistic personality.

QUEER DECOYS

Radclyffe Hall explicitly links the logorrheic artistic personality back to Wildean dandyism, effeminacy, and homosexuality in her 1928 lesbian novel *The Well of Loneliness*, but it does so in the interest of a queer ethics that surpasses the pleasures of style for style's sake. One of the most important characters in the novel, a gay man named Jonathan Brockett based on the real-life Noel Coward, befriends the novel's lesbian protagonist Stephen Gordon, convinces her to move to Paris, and introduces her to Natalie Barney, thinly disguised in the novel as the salonnière Valerie Seymour. Brockett is the only character in the story to speak at length, and in this rather dignified novel, his speech stands out—as he does—like a sore thumb. Brockett's chattiness, however, not only is his signature style, but it performs a queer ethics of care as well, creating community through his dramatization of queer identity for other gay men and lesbians. In this portrait—arguably the most overt literary portrait of male homosexuality since the Wilde trials thirty-three years earlier—Brockett's camp style reveals itself as a dynamic social ethic, one that solicits the gaze and acts as a decoy in the service of a larger good:

> And now he was launched on a torrent of gossip about people of whom Stephen had never even heard: "Pat's been deserted—have you heard that, darling? Do you think she'll take the veil or cocaine or something? One never quite knows what may happen next with such an emotional temperament, does one? Arabella's skipped off to the Lido with Jane Grigg. The Grigg's just come into pots and pots of money, so I hope they'll be deliriously happy and silly while it lasts—I mean the money. . . . Oh, and have you heard about Rachel Morris? They say . . ." He flowed on and on like a brook in spring flood, while Valerie yawned and looked bored, making monosyllabic answers.[13]

Speaking style signals one's relation to inversion in *The Well;* here Brockett's flow of words signals his verbose effeminacy, in contrast with Stephen's and Valerie's more masculine taciturnity. But Brockett's urgent style of speaking is also both stylish and anxious, making a style out of anxiety and suggesting the anguish at the root of his verbal proficiency. He is eager to have interactions go smoothly, and he willingly plays the queeny buffoon in order to draw ridicule to himself and thus make everyone else comfortable by comparison. No one has to feel embarrassed for him since he preemptively solicits the attention he is bound to draw anyway, then plays with that attention in such a way as to assert his control over its censure and his contempt for it.

The narrator seems often not to understand the strategy of Brockett's style, and alternates between shuddering at his effeminacy and conceding his good intentions:

> And Stephen as she sat there and smoked in silence, thought grimly: "This is all being said because of me. Brockett wants to let me see that he knows what I am, and he wants to let Valerie Seymour know too—I suppose this is making me welcome." She hardly knew whether to feel outraged or relieved that here, at least, was no need for pretences. (247)

Stephen rejects his mannerisms as abnormal, unnatural, and an affront to masculinity, yet Stephen's ambivalent response to these mannerisms is also the way the text tracks her journey to queer acceptance and solidarity. Brockett's words—and the words of other gay men who confront Stephen in the text—force her to reconsider the ways in which she participates in her own silencing, as well as in the silencing of others. His perverse affectation reveals Stephen to herself through her reaction to both his abnormality and his kindness, showing both the difference and distance between comportment and character, and the queer ethics of allowing them to collapse into each other as part of a social project of engendering uneasiness with the conventions and values of normativity. The ambivalence that Brockett plants in Stephen's conventional opinions bears fruit later in the novel when she is confronted by a drug addict who demands that she see him and recognize their kinship. In a seedy underworld bar frequented by drug dealers and addicts, homosexual men, lesbians, alcoholics, prostitutes, defrocked priests, and other social outcasts, she is forced to shift alliances, or at least to see the necessity of doing so:

> He bent forward, this youth, until his face was almost on a level with Stephen's—a grey, drug-marred face with a mouth that trembled incessantly.
>
> "Ma soeur," he whispered.
>
> For a moment she wanted to strike that face with her naked fist, to obliterate it. Then all of a sudden she perceived the eyes and the memory came of a hapless creature, distracted, bleeding from bursting lungs, hopelessly pursued, glancing this way, then that, as though looking for something, some refuge, some hope—and the thought: "It's looking for God who made it."
>
> Stephen shivered and stared at her tightly clenched hands; the nails whitened her flesh. "Mon frère," she muttered. (394)

Brockett's self-conscious chatter now characterizes the monologue inside Stephen's head, but this time the words are hers. Internalizing his run-on style, she internalizes his message of ethical affiliation, admitting her kinship with the people she habitually despises. This kinship makes her suffer a kind of crucifixion—the "nails" she drives into her palms—but it also makes her less primitive, dark, and sexual according to the racial schematic of the novel, as it "whiten[s] her flesh." The ambivalence produced by Brockett's logorrhea thus forces Stephen's unconscious to become more present and exposes the ideological underpinnings of her culture in such a way as to reveal them as unacceptable, if not to Stephen, then to the readers of *The Well* who might easily identify such attitudes as the chief source of Stephen's sexual and gender misery.

Jonathan Brockett assumes the persona of the chattering sissy in order to make others feel comfortable by drawing negative attention to himself, and this assumption of hypervisibility performs the function of decoy or scapegoat. But hypervisibility can also assume a majestic dignity, a dignity far grander than the humility of Christian martyrs Hall's text offers to extend to self-sacrificing homosexuals. The homosexual transvestite doctor Matthew O'Connor in Djuna Barnes's 1936 *Nightwood,* arguably the most famous queer logorrheac in modernism, is also the most diva-esque, a persona that approaches camp in his tawdry excessiveness, but whose misery works against reading with any measure of ironic distance. Matthew's talking hijacks the novel halfway through and only reluctantly gives up control at the end of *Nightwood,* when the narrative wrenches itself away from him to follow the tragic lesbians Robin Vote and Nora Flood once more. Like Jonathan Brockett, Matthew produces discourse with an ethics, though in his case it is for the opposite purpose. His weariness with talking expresses cynicism over the ability of talking to do anything, and by extension, modernism and modernist style become useless. No one really hears what he is saying, although they all want to listen to him, or at least observe his performance as a curiosity and an entertainment:

> People had begun to whisper and the waiters moved closer, watching. The ex-priest was smiling to himself, but O'Connor did not seem to see or hear anything but his own heart. "Some people," he said, "take off head-first into *any* body of water and six glasses later someone in Haarlem gets typhoid from drinking their misery. God, take my hand and get me up out of this great argument—the more you go against your nature, the more you will know of it—hear me, Heaven! I've done and been everything that I didn't want to be or do—Lord, put the light out—so I stand here, beaten up and mauled and weeping, knowing I am not what I thought I was, a good man doing wrong, but the wrong man doing nothing much, and I wouldn't be telling you about it if I weren't talking to myself. I talk too much because I have been made miserable by what you are keeping hushed."[14]

The text makes O'Connor a babbling hysteric whose talking stages his identity as the symptom of his culture's hypocrisy and repression. His words have no rhetorical situation, no audience or purpose or argument (he says), but are meant to flood the space between secrecy and truth. He is merely confessional, though he does name names as well, a highly annoying trait, mostly because we get the point of his character right away, though the novel allows him to go on and on and on. His *Yellow Book* rhetoric, so like the Wildean language found in that aesthetic manifesto, resonates with hopelessness and drunken self-pity. Why does the text render him as such a spectacle of Cassandra-like impotence, as a talker worth watching but not hearing?

As the last gasp of a queerly logorrheic modernism, O'Connor's exhaustion undercuts the polymorphous playfulness of the best modernist monologues, lacking the gentleness with which even Prufrock cuts his habit of ironic self-distancing. But this exhaustion stands in relation to his belligerent insistence on his own presence, on his own existence and right to existence. The spectacle of O'Connor is crucial to his presence, his character, and the way all the novel becomes his portrait, and his portrait condenses all the novel. O'Connor's parable of the water emphasizes how related everyone everywhere is to each other. How is it that you think you are not me? he asks. As readers recoil, perhaps, from the harshness of his language and the tiresomeness of his drunken dogmatism, they also encounter this voice that rebukes their impulse to turn away. This voice that will not be silenced, the voice that he claims contains all the repression of his society, finally creates its own dignity in indignity through nothing more than testimony, confrontation, and the stubborn refusal to be discreet. Logorrhea here refuses any curb as complicit with the silencing impulses of sexual respectability, though it also recognizes the complicity of talking with social control:

> I've given my destiny away by garrulity, like ninety per cent of everybody else—for, no matter what I may be doing, in my heart is the wish for children and knitting. God, I never asked better than to boil some good man's potatoes and toss up a child for him every nine months by the calendar. Is it my fault that my only fireside is the outhouse? And that I can never hang my muffler, mittens and Bannybrook umbrella on anything better than a bit of tin boarding as high as my eyes, having to be brave, no matter what, to keep the mascara from running away? (91)

Here is also the outhouse aesthetic of Gide and Genet, the locus of social marginality rendered spatially as the place where lost and prohibited sensual and sexual experiences can be recovered and indulged. This place is only available to O'Connor in talk, where he spins out the connections between his domestic and domesticated yearnings at the same time as their very articulation marks them as impossibly queer. To give one's destiny away is here both to make it impossible for one's self to have it, yet at the same time make it possible for another, someone listening or reading, who hears about it and imagines it for herself as an alternative to sexual convention, enclosure, and silence.

MADAM TALKS BACK

> My name is Johnson—
> Madam Alberta K.
> The Madam stands for business.
> I'm smart that way.[15]

So speaks the sassy persona of Langston Hughes's "Madam" poems, Alberta K.Johnson, who proves herself a much more effective rhetorician than Barnes's Matthew O'Connor. Madam is a striking character, one Arnold Rampersad calls "an instantly recognizable Harlem type despite her memorable individuality."[16] She is also a powerful older woman, a Madam rather than a Miss, whose own voice delights her and whose character clearly fascinated the black gay poet who invented her in 1943 and used her in at least eighteen of his poems.[17] Madam also tells her life story to the interlocutors who confront her and question her status and dignity by invoking institutions and bourgeois normativity. Her persecutors demand her life story and her rent, question her phone bill, her status as a citizen, and her religious salvation. At every turn she is asked to account for herself. Her position as the subject of involuntary interrogation does not, however, produce the kind of confession that fixes or pathologizes her. Instead, her response is always to turn the question back upon whoever attempts to scrutinize her and find her wanting. Unlike O'Connor, who wears his social abjection as a proud badge of misery, Madam talks back by riffing off the accusations or normative demands her interrogators use to question her, building her own argument to counter theirs by using wordplay—rhyme, double entendres, repetition, sarcasm, and sometimes outright opposition.

This wordplay helps her build a haughty, powerfully feminine identity, and is at the same time an expression of that identity, one that refuses to take advantage of heterosexual privilege, refuses to give up her dignity even in the face of love, refuses to be humiliated by bill collectors, and turns the tables on those who try to make her feel powerless by sarcastically interrogating the terms other people use to characterize the demands they make on her pride and her resources. In "Madam's Past History" she tells the story of losing a hairdressing business in the Depression, losing a barbecue stand because of an unscrupulous boyfriend, and being told that in spite of her financial hardship she could not qualify for the WPA because she had an insurance policy. Instead of folding, however, she harnesses her self-respect and proudly declares herself to be a woman of both substance and stature:

I said,
DON'T WORRY 'BOUT ME!
Just like the song,
You WPA folks take care of yourself—
And I'll get along.

I do cooking,
Day's work, too!
Alberta K. Johnson—
Madam to you. (18–26)

This persona builds from her insistence on her own independence and worth, an insistence that seems to rise out of the rhyming assertions of her argument: "Just like the song . . . I'll get along!" When she caps her speech by naming herself as a lady—"*Madam* to you"—it is the culmination of all of the good qualities of survival she knows make her too powerful to be beaten down, either by hard times, men, or the government. "Madam" is a self who turns suffering into strength, and she demonstrates that strength as something powerful enough to reconfigure language, words, and other people's misguided notions of her. Her incantatory, bluesy speeches enjoy their own inventiveness even as they demonstrate her power and worth as a resourceful and creative woman, as well as an artist of words.

Indeed, Alberta often shows that being a woman, being strong, and being an artist are all interrelated for her. In "Madam and the Phone Bill" she tries to convince the phone company that she shouldn't have to pay the bill for a romantic relationship that is now long over:

You say I O.K.ed
LONG DISTANCE?
O.K.ed it when?
My goodness, Central,
That was *then!*

I'm mad and disgusted
With that Negro now.
I don't pay no REVERSED
CHARGES nohow. (1–9)

Madam's argument imagines a corporate America—a Central—that forgives phone bills according to its interest in facilitating relationships that do not fail. Madam's utopian desire for a corporate state system that would not make you pay for phone calls to a former lover ironically underscores how the system remains indifferent to love and to lovers of all kinds.

In "Madam and the Rent Man" Alberta confronts the rental agent's demand for money with a litany of complaints that crescendos to a full-blown tenant's bill of rights:

> I said, Listen,
> Before I'd pay
> I'd go to Hades
> And rot away!
>
> The sink is broke,
> The water don't run,
> And you ain't done a thing
> You promised to've done.
>
> Back window's cracked,
> Kitchen floor squeaks,
> There's rats in the cellar,
> And the attic leaks. (7–18)

She takes his demand and adds her own list of demands, drafting a social contract where nobody gets what they want until everybody gets what they want. Every word she uses to make a rhyme seems to add power to her complaint, and her pleasure in the growing conviction of her position finds its triumph when the agent addresses her as "Madam":

> He said, Madam,
> It's not up to me.
> I'm just the agent,
> Don't you see? (19–22)

For him "Madam" is a generic term, one he uses to try to coerce her. He emphasizes her generic identity—she is just Madam so-and-so to him—

and his own benign status as an employee without accountability in an attempt to get her to agree to an alienated transaction. But Madam Alberta is only fueled by the pleasure of her own inventive haughtiness by his address, which she takes as a recognition of her authority as "Madam":

> I said, Naturally,
> You pass the buck.
> If it's money you want
> You're out of luck.

> He said, Madam,
> I ain't pleased!
> I said, Neither am I.

> So we agrees! (23–30)

What is remarkable about Madam's speech is both her enormous confidence in the righteousness of her position and the litany that seems to gather strength from its own inventive power as her complaint builds. When the rental agent addresses her finally as "Madam" in a vain attempt to convince her that his displeasure matters, she turns his meaning around to agree with hers and ends by asserting her "I." Unmoved and unbowed, she wins the argument by pointing out their common ground, not only in agreeing to disagree, but insofar as neither of them agrees with the positions of the absent landlord who exploits them both. Madam, however, actively resists, while the rental agent passively "pass[es] the buck." The agent proves to be no agent at all, but by finding a point of common agreement between herself and the agent, dramatizing the unfairness of the landlord's demand for rent, drafting a bill of rights where landlords only get paid when they take good care of their tenants, and insisting on her own power to represent herself with eloquence, dignity, and inventiveness, Madam offers him a point of agreement upon which resistance to the system might be possible, and community might be formed between people of seemingly disparate interests.

I have tried to suggest that logorrheic modernism talks back by dramatizing the seeming pathology and social inconsequentiality of the abnormal, effeminate chatterer. Stream-of-consciousness narration that becomes streaming talk not only ventriloquizes the manic anxiety of the modern era while insisting on the right of queer characters to speak, but also talks back with chatter, prattle, gossip, mimicry, haughtiness, and a self-consciously theatrical stage patter that dramatizes abnormality, anxiety, effeminacy, and queerness. Logorrheic modernism takes up the weapons of a stagey, dignified femininity that refuses to back down or relinquish the scolding, inventive, punning, rapping, protean powers of language. Mobilizing character and peculiarity, it insists on particularity and queerness, but particularity in the context of oppression, social injustice, particularity that cannot take refuge in individualism—the privileges of Stephen's aristocracy, or the benign compliance of Madam's rent man—but speaks as a queer act of participation in language, and insists on a larger and more just social world.

Romaine Brooks (1874–1970). © Copyright. *Una, Lady Troubridge*. Oil on canvas, 1924. Smithsonian American Art Museum, Washington, DC, U.S.A. Brooks's portrait of Radclyffe Hall's lover Una Troubridge with their dogs was viewed by many as bordering on caricature, but Troubridge's monocle also emphasizes the sitter's gaze back out at the artist and spectators. Photo credit: Smithsonian American Art Museum, Washington, DC / Art Resource, NY

3

Caricature Studies

What's so funny about lesbians? In modernism, apparently a great deal. In 1928 alone three satires appeared about lesbians: Compton Mackenzie's *Extraordinary Women*, Djuna Barnes's *Ladies Almanack*, and Virginia Woolf's *Orlando*. In addition, Wyndham Lewis's 1930 *The Apes of God*, which skewers homosexual men and women with equal vigor, has a chapter called "Lesbian-Ape" that uses comic conventions of mistaken identity and mutual gender and sexual suspicion to send up the queer genders of mannish women and effeminate men. Other and more serious portraits of lesbians, such as Radclyffe Hall's *The Well of Loneliness*, were followed by satires, such as *The Sink of Solitude*. These comic portraits by women and men about lesbians and gay men respond to modernism's perverse portraiture by focusing squarely on sexual and gender deviants. They show modernism contemplating itself, they send up the pretensions and dramas of postwar bohemianism, and—most importantly—their satiric and sometimes savage stance further torques the twisted gaze of literary portraiture. In these portraits caricature foregrounds the constraining, biased nature of the look, but its conventions also enable those who are seen to appropriate its looking, and to look back.

As we have seen earlier, theatrical self-consciousness is perverse in its refusal of the look, and in its insistence that the look can be twisted around, turned back on itself, and subverted. Lacan saw subjects attempting to escape the limitation of being looked at—and with it, the sense of being inscribed within sexual difference—through forms of self-consciousness and theatrical self-presentation that reclaim the objects of perception as part of the subject's illusion of coherence and self-mastery. The interwar satirical portraits I discuss in this chapter recognize the impersonations, poses, and disguises that subjects use to subvert the look and take great delight in exposing these to ridicule. Satirical portraits of modernist-era homosexual men and women—no matter how sympathetic—often, though not always, domesticate their subjects. They show, or attempt to show, the inescapable nature of the gaze. Wyndham Lewis famously called his satire a "philosophy of the EYE."[1] The delight some modernist satires take in piercing the layers of disguise, affectation, impersonation, and self-importance that lend their targets the illusion of dignity is itself a reaction to the queerly theatrical self-fashioning of modernist portraiture, which refuses to be "taken down" by the look.

Another strategy of the satirical portraits of the era is to turn the satirical look itself in another direction. As Hugh Kenner points out in an essay on Wyndham Lewis, satire is a "radically *written* genre,"[2] and this means the nature of its critique will be systemic. It will to some extent interrogate the larger social order that creates the grotesques it studies, as well as lampooning the grotesques that are the subject of its humor. Satires such as Wyndham Lewis's *Apes of God* and Compton Mackenzie's *Extraordinary Women* uphold the normativity of the look that depends on this split; by contrast, Djuna Barnes's *Ladies Almanack* and Virginia Woolf's *Orlando* turn the satiric look back on both hetero- and homonormativity, implicating the norms satire uses for its effects. Satire's ability to whirl about and pull the rug out from under the norms upon which its critique is built is nowhere better exploited than in Barnes's *Almanack*, perhaps the era's most subversive satire. Although some of the lesbian satires of the era domesticate their subjects, *Almanack* turns the look queerly around, producing as it does so one of the most stylistically original texts in all of modernism. By closing the distance between the subjects of satire and the narrative voice, the narrator of the *Almanack* exploits the queer doubleness at the heart of satire, its ability to bite the hand of the social mores that feed it, emphasizing, in the process, the rich wildness of lesbian desire, embodiment, and sexuality. What becomes really funny is not so much the freakishness of lesbians as it is the narrowness of the conventional views held by the people who misunderstand them. Virginia Woolf's *Orlando* also tweaks the satiric look, but it does so ambivalently, displacing the sexual and gender abnormality of its mannish women and androgynous men onto foreigners and non-Anglo racial "others." Modernist satirical portraits thus exaggerate the split between seeing and being looked at that emphasizes the normative and controlling look, but they also make fun of the very same look they use to make their critique, undoing its status.

Lewis's *Apes of God* represents perhaps the most conventional kind of satire in terms of the relationship between its subject and its frame. Its subjects are all exaggerated types; the narrator is especially pitiless in exposing both feminine pretension and gender traits that seem inappropriately queer. The "Lesbian-Ape" chapter follows the exploits of the hapless, effeminate Dan as he mistakenly wanders into a "great nest of women Apes"[3] and confronts a creature too masculine to be male:

> With alarm he glanced up. Before him stood a severe masculine figure. In general effect it was a bavarian youth-movement elderly enthusiast. She was beyond question somewhat past mark-of-mouth. But this was a woman, as in fact she had appeared in the typed description. Of that he felt tolerably certain, because of the indefinable something that could only be described as "masculine." An heroic something or other in the bold blue eye, that held an eyeglass, that reminded him of the Old Guard or the Death-or-Glory-Boys, in the house of Mr. Brian Macdonnell, secured for him certainty of the sex at least without further worry. It was She. This was Miss Ansell. (234)

Exaggeration distances the narrator from the scene and creates humor; she is not only masculine, she is downright militaristic. Offered without the intervention of commentary or opinion, the narrator's rendering of Dan's reasoning is rather startling: this world has grown so topsy-turvy that masculinity is a sure sign that one is facing a woman. The straight-faced delivery of this information makes the satire doubly "comic" if you like your humor on the homophobic side. The arch and sophisticated narrator is perfectly aware of what is going on, and in assuming it to be perfectly natural, invokes readers' reactive intolerant response—this is *not* natural—in order to achieve an effect. Thus the narrator escapes seeming conventional while relying on his audience to be so. The text produces the humor that reacts against the supposition that these gender inversions are normal precisely by refusing to be outraged, yet soliciting outrage through grotesque exaggeration and deadpan narration.

Men as well as women are the butt of the novel's ridicule, if they are "abnormal" types. There is no more hapless character in modernism than the skittering sissy Dan, who shrieks at the sight of lesbians, moons over handsome men, flees the caresses of women, and is earnestly pursued by both men and women eager to enjoy his charms and fashion his tastes. An aesthetic innocent, he first wanders into the lesbian's den because he has been sent to the wrong address to be an artist's model. In another moment, he is harangued in a letter by a man named Horace Zagreus, who flatters Dan by calling him a genius and offers to mentor him in language that is both overblown and oddly pornographic: "I solicit the privilege of being your gardener at this crisis, oh delicate moon-flower" (125).

Accompanying this letter is a long treatise by a "painter turned philosopher" (138) named Pierpoint denouncing the dilettantism of wealthy dabblers in the arts, whom he christens "Apes of God" (131). At this point it seems as if both the predatory Zagreus and his crackpot mentor Pierpoint will become objects of the text's ridicule, as Zagreus's designs on Dan are clearly exploitative, and Pierpoint's aesthetic rantings are not only vociferous, but lengthy, haughty, and self-righteous. Yet the satire turns away from satirizing the satirist, and instead goes on to place the blame for apishness on the sexual and gender deviancy of these residents of "Paris . . . Chelsea, Bloomsbury, and Mayfair" (131). Pierpoint's treatise defines "Apes of God" as sexual and gender freaks whose sinfulness lies in the excessiveness with which they display themselves as insincere, theatrical personalities:

> It is to what I have called Apes of God that I am drawing your attention—*those prosperous mountebanks who alternately imitate and mock at and traduce those figures they at once admire and hate.* And bringing against such individuals and their productions all the artillery of the female, or bi-sexual tongue, will abuse the object of their envy one day, and imitate him the next: will attempt to identify themselves with him in people's minds, but in the same breath attempt to belittle him—to lessen if possible the disadvantage for them that this neighborhood will reveal. I will make them parade before you in their borrowed plumes like mannequins, spouting their trite tags, and you shall judge if my account is true. (131; original italics)

Pierpoint is a crackpot, but his theories are certainly no less ridiculous than the spectacle of queer bohemianism he describes, or that which the novel shows. Dan rolls his "lovely" eyes and becomes precisely the kind of ape Pierpoint describes, *"the-genius-without-a-studio"* (138; original italics) who believes Zagreus's flattering description of his genius. Dan's maternal friend Melanie, a painter who recognizes herself in Pierpoint's description but perversely insists on trying to seduce the queer "Dandarling"—as she insists on calling him—is equally ridiculous in her smocks, painting bright pictures and needling Dan with her flirtatious sexual innuendos. These apes are condemned by the text as misguided in their belief in their own talents, and insincere—and therefore, silly—in their insistent playfulness and self-invention. Apishness is perverse in that it cannot distinguish between authentic artistry and willful bohemian pretensions, and thus Lewis insists on a genuine artistic identity and savagely attacks the narcissistic pleasures of queer creative aspiration for its own sake: "He was going to Horace Zagreus, who believed in his *genius!*" (139). As its title suggests, *Apes of God* installs the eye in the text as a fixed and regulating look, one that condemns role-playing and self-invention as mere posturing and therefore stands above "Being-as-Playing-a-Role," and one that, as a result, shuts down the pleasure of soliciting looking, being seen, and looking at one's self being seen that informs the most self-conscious and best modernist portraits.

ORDINARY WOMEN

Whereas Lewis's text wants to get rid of the threat posed by gender inversion by encouraging readers to laugh masculine women and effeminate men out of town, Compton Mackenzie's *Extraordinary Women* is much more sympathetic, domesticating the "mythic, mannish lesbian" by feminizing her and rendering her impotent. "Rosalba was a portent," the narrator relates, but then seems unable to decide what exactly is meant by this. "Of what is Rosalba the portent? What signifies this boy-girl at whom all the clumsy Swiss are staring on this fine May morning? What signifies she in the curve of a civilization?"[4] These questions remain unanswered: we are given only to understand that "Her profile was Greek in the way that Virgil's hexameters are Greek," and that "Her mouth curved up at the corners like the mouths Leonardo da Vinci loved to paint" (41). Rosalba is not so much a portent here as a throwback; she recalls Sappho's classical Greece not in her ethnicity but in her approximation of a physical ideal the narrator associates with Greece. At the same time she seems to embody the Renaissance; her smile is the smile of the Mona Lisa, and of John the Baptist. Yet her "boy-girl" nature is clearly something new despite her classical aspect; it renders the Teutonic Swiss "clumsy" and outmoded, and seems to point civilization in a new direction.

In this way, *Extraordinary Women* makes lesbians harmless by making them the quintessential figures of "modernism." Like most of the era's avant-garde and experimental writing, these lesbians are grounded in the classical Western tradition; like textual modernisms, they are supposed to remake that tradition for the future. Rosalba may strut like a man in collar and evening shirt, but she looks like the Mona Lisa. The novel does something similar with lesbian society on the island of Sirene. They may look like a bunch of terrifying abnormal women, but their world is merely a gossipy den of intrigue, with the same plots and counterplots one might expect to find in female society, which by definition should be more preoccupied with love and domestic drama than politics. The eye of the narrator fixes these women as objects of scrutiny, as portents, as art. There is reason to fix them as objects of scrutiny because they are strange, interesting, abnormal. But they are also women, and in emphasizing their feminine aspects, the text neutralizes their difference:

> Rosalba cheered things up. That was her justification in the eyes of the Sirenesi. Accustomed for years to the spectacle of ladylike men they were not capable of being shocked by gentlemanly women. They ascribed the phenomenon of Rosalba and her friends to the war. "Poor women," they said, "there is a scarcity of men." Rosalba was beautiful, and the Sirenesi living as they did in the Bay of Naples disliked ugliness. (134)

While the text lampoons the philosophical and aesthetic views of its lesbian characters, it does so gently, even to the point of letting those views stand on their own merits. The effect is strangely tolerant, and at times the narrator seems to agree more with the characters than with any contrary point of view the so-called normal world might hold:

> [Olimpia] imagined a race of homosexual men and women who would in the course of time exhaust the physical expression of sexuality through atrophy caused by the repeated futility of a sterile act. The instinct of sublimation would thus be refreshed, and finally there would be achieved a race of creative minds which had completely mastered the body. She did not accept such a race as the equivalent of any third sex at present imagined. (231)

At other moments the text is more firmly in control of its "normal" point of view:

> These dinner-parties of Rosalba's had little in common with that form of entertainment as it is usually practised among civilized communities. They partook more of the nature of seances at which everybody is wrought up to a pitch of nervous tension and expectation. The mere passing of the salt or pepper involved as much expense of emotion as an elegy of Propertius. All life's fever was in a salad bowl. A heart bled

when a glass was filled with wine. We know what an atmosphere can be created at a dinner-party by one jealous woman. At Rosalba's parties there were often eight women, the palpitations of whose hidden jealousies, baffled desires and wounded vanities was in its influence upon the ambient air as potent as the dreadful mustering of subterranean fires before an eruption. (263)

The normative frame of reference here is "civilized communities." In these, the narrative implies, all life's fever is *not* in a salad bowl, and this is due to fewer jealous women all in one place. In the uncivilized society of the narrative, the concentration of women is too high, and thus the drama is amplified to an unbearable degree. But it is not the abnormal sexuality of these women that makes their society uncivilized; it is simply that there are too many women. They are not frightening so much as they are ridiculous, comic, hysterical, female.

Finally Rosalba leaves the island, abandoning her long-suffering admirer Rory Freemantle to the company of the sissy "Cissie" Daffodil. Together they drink tea and think of England: "There was no escaping it. She *was* longing for a cup of tea as ardently as thousands and thousands of ordinary women at home in England were at this very moment longing for their cups of tea. Daffodil flung himself down into a chair and gave her the Piazza news while they waited for the chink of crockery" (391–92). In this final, cozy scene, the effeminate homosexual man and the mannish lesbian become just another couple enjoying the simple pleasures of domesticity. Their pleasure in tea, home, and each other becomes an English pleasure, one that grounds their identities in exile, among other sexual, national, and gender exiles, as quintessentially normal.

RHETORICAL MASQUERADE[5]

Virginia Woolf's satiric *roman à clef*, *Orlando*, whose protagonist changes gender across several centuries and continents, also domesticates lesbians by emphasizing their traditional presence in English literature, in the aristocracy, and in the English nation and empire. While the novel uses racially and sexually "foreign" subjects to explore the ambiguous national and social identity of a queerly gendered white Englishwoman, *Orlando*'s jocular but insistent production of a femininity rendered as white also allows the novel's protagonist to "pass" as respectable and heterosexual by displacing her transgressive sexuality onto racial others, masking Orlando's masculine-identified literary and sexual desires. As readers have long observed, costume as one form of masquerade allows the protagonist of Woolf's novel to play with gender roles. The construction of its lesbian protagonist's polymorphous sexual desire as an exotic fantasy may also have helped *Orlando* slip past the censors who banned Radclyffe Hall's deadly serious, stolidly identitarian lesbian novel for describing "certain acts . . . in the most alluring terms."[6] *Orlando* continues, by authorial decree, to be read as an inside joke; Woolf's oft-cited journal entries have encouraged this reading of her literary "sapphism" as a cheerful "wildness," as a masquerade that allows her the freedom "to kick up [her] heels and be off."[7] Indeed, humor operates as another kind of masquerade in the novel. As Pamela Caughie points out, rhetoric stands with fashion, gender, and genre as one of the chief "signifying systems" the novel uses to make—and question—meaning.[8]

From the very start of *Orlando*, the narrating Biographer steadies Orlando's indeterminate gender by articulating his masculinity within the racialized terms of national identity:

> He—for there could be no doubt of his sex, though the fashion of the time did something to disguise it—was in the act of slicing at the head of a Moor which swung at the rafters. It was the colour of an old football, and more or less the shape of one, save for the sunken cheeks and a strand or two of coarse, dry hair, like the hair on a cocoanut. Orlando's father, or perhaps his grandfather, had struck it from the head of a vast pagan who had started up under the moon in the barbarian fields of Africa; and now it swung, gently, perpetually, in the breeze which never ceased blowing through the attic rooms of the gigantic house of the lord who had slain him.[9]

The "he" in this opening paragraph is a masquerading subject whose gender indeterminacy is displaced as a textual question by the description of the Moor's head. The "fashion" of the time—a phrase that suggests not only clothes but also customs and mores—disguises his sex, which, however, the Biographer insists cannot be in doubt precisely because Orlando's display of valor puts his masculinity beyond question. Indeed, the Biographer takes pains to allay any suspicions one might have about Orlando's gender identity by admiring Orlando's iterative performance of masculine militarism. The Biographer reassures the reader that Orlando's behavior repeats that of his English forefathers; Orlando's play is thus simultaneously consistent with "his" masculinity, that of his father, and the feudal service demanded of him by his nation and his queen. By miming masculine imperialism, Orlando literally engenders the narrative that bears his name, commences as the novel's protagonist, and enters the social and symbolic fields as a national subject.

Yet Woolf's text undermines the chauvinistic certainty it appears to create. The narrator's joking tone remains ambivalent, performing a delicate balancing act throughout the novel which juxtaposes both a critique of Orlando and a celebration of him. Her sarcastic rendering of Orlando's racialized masculinity questions the terms that valorize his behavior as a gendered national ideal. The text's claim that Orlando demonstrates "chivalry" in hanging the head almost out of his own reach appears doubtful given that his Anglo-Saxon manhood emerges as the result of a fixed fight against a long-dead "enemy." Indeed, the opening spectacle of the Moor's repeated demise at the hands of England's young heirs, his head little more than "an old football" (1), suggests that colonial conquest is both a rite of passage and a sign of immaturity. Orlando seems, on the one hand, to embody the popular phrase "vigorous, manly and English," yet Orlando and his head-hunting forefathers also appear to be far more barbaric than the singularly uninspiring Moor, whose disembodied visage serves as a perpetual reminder of the violent appropriations that built the wealth and identity of "gigantic" houses such as that of the Sackvilles.

Rhetorical masquerades, such as the foregrounding of biographical and historical methodology, textual "double-dealing" (as Freud might call it), and narrative coyness, continue to construct Orlando's sexuality as fundamentally ambiguous when s/he changes gender. While serving as an English governor in Constantinople, Orlando adopts the clothes and customs of his new city, has an affair with a gypsy woman, and becomes a "she." Since it is never clear whether Orlando becomes female before, during, or after her affair with the gypsy woman, the sexual configuration of their relationship remains murky. The dearth of biographical information during Orlando's sojourn in Constantinople suggests that Orlando's "queering" of his/her national and gender identity obfuscates his national role: "We have done our best," the Biographer insists, "to piece out a meagre summary from the charred fragments that remain; but often it has been necessary to speculate, to surmise, and even to make use of the imagination." Because Orlando's incongruent gender (she "becomes" a woman) and sexual object-choice (during an affair with a woman) means that she is neither English nor a "lady" in the eyes of respectable British society, she is rendered in the text as a biographical puzzle and an unintelligible exile. Although the Biographer states that

Orlando "had become" a woman, the narrative also slyly implies, with a great deal of pronoun juxtapositioning, that Orlando has been some combination of both sexes for some time: "we have no choice but to confess—he was a woman." The pronoun play continues even after this confession, when the now-female Orlando "looked himself up and down in a long looking-glass, without showing any signs of discomposure." This is the first time that Orlando appears naked; the mirror, the masculine "he," and the narrator's apologetic reassurance that subsequent pronoun substitutions are "for convention's sake" all suggest that Orlando is and has always been masquerading.

Woolf's novel critiques Orlando's acquiescence to the compulsory heterosexuality and lesbian invisibility of Englishness by humorously suggesting that Orlando's subsequent longing for a husband is unhealthy for her body, leading to neurasthenic bouts of mania and lethargy. Heterosexual marriage is not only "against her natural temperament" but also, as the text slyly implies, highly artificial, in that it "did not seem to be [of] Nature." In a hallucination that startles Orlando one day in her carriage, she sees the "heterogeneous" symbols and spoils of Victorian culture's "garish erection" being propped up by a bourgeois heterosexual couple in the drag of absolute gender difference, "the whole supported like a gigantic coat of arms on the right side by a female figure clothed in flowing white; on the left, by a portly gentleman wearing a frock-coat and sponge-bag trousers." Orlando's "banquet-table" vision intuits the interrelatedness of heterosexual respectability, bourgeois consumption, and imperial expansion. The woman's gendered yet sexless moral purity is linked to a whiteness that makes disappear the body beneath it, while the man's expansive physique and business costume together suggest the gluttonous disposition required of the capitalist. Both gender roles operate as national and nationalist costumes, as the "coat of arms" suggests. Although Orlando struggles to look away, she passes Buckingham Palace at that very moment, notices that she is herself cross-dressing in breeches, and, feeling that her lack of femininity has shamed her before the queen, "never ceased blushing till she had reached her country house."

Orlando and her husband Shelmerdine's participation in the cultural values of empire—this "indecent" monument—means that they uphold fictions of national belonging that are tied to fictions of racial belonging and heterosexual, middle-class respectability. The novel's displacement of perverse desires onto the exotic "other" suggests that both Orlando and Shel understand that sexual sustenance may lie outside the bounds of a bourgeois and heterosexually monogamous English respectability:

> [H]e went to the top of the mast in a gale; there reflected on the destiny of man; came down again; had a whiskey and soda; went on shore; was trapped by a black woman; repented; reasoned it out; read Pascal; determined to write philosophy. . . . All this and a thousand other things she understood him to say and so when she replied, Yes, negresses are seductive, aren't they? he having told her that his supply of biscuits now gave out, he was surprised and delighted to find how well she had taken his meaning.

Orlando's and Shelmerdine's snappy repartee masks their discussion of sexual tastes as a conversation about travel adventures. The "negress" in their exchange signifies sexual perversity and ambivalent gender identification, with a racially and nationally colonized figure discursively appropriated to mark the closeting of Orlando's and Shel's queerness by a national respectability.

Wary of censorship, the Biographer maintains that such double entendres are necessary as "the main art of speech in an age when words are growing daily so scanty in comparison with ideas that 'the biscuits ran out' has to stand for kissing a negress in the dark." Assenting to the cultural values that exoticize their homosexual, interracial, and cross-class sexual tastes, Orlando and Shelmerdine agree to closet their sexuality, to kiss their unacceptable sexual objects—their "negresses"—in the dark. The text satirizes their smug agreement that secrecy intensifies pleasure; clearly, the logic of their reasoning makes no apparent sense. Yet their delight in each other, their willingness to confess all between them, also challenges traditional notions of married fidelity. Indeed, their frankness with each other in sexual matters throws essential gender into doubt: "Are you positive you aren't a man?" he asks, and she replies, "Can it be possible you're not a woman?" Shelmerdine reads Orlando's sympathetic understanding of his desire for "negresses" in two ways: she is both tolerant of his desires *and* shares them, to the point of having a masculine identification. However, in adopting his racialized erotic language to serve as an intimate language between the two of them, Orlando offers up her own masculinity and gender ambiguity to a white and heterosexual national respectability. Further, because the "negress" in *Orlando* operates as a textual code, she is also exchanged with Woolf's readers as a sign of gender play. The Biographer, asserting that "only the most profound masters of style can tell the truth," defends this transparent doubleness as instructive. The vocabulary of colonial national and sexual masculine conquest of the racial "other" that the text uses to convey their mutual understanding also enables Woolf's Biographer to indicate "the truth" that this narrative style conceals.

As these earlier images suggest, the "negress" in the text operates not as a referent but as a symbol of an ambiguous gender and sexuality. Shelmerdine's and Orlando's masquerade and triangulation of desire through the exotic "negress" reconfigure the first violent image of the Moor's head, domesticating the dynamics of imperialism and violent conquest into primitivist and orientalist style. Indeed, Orlando's respectable marriage allows her to write overtly sapphic hymns to the charms of "Egyptian girls" without censure. When the voice of the age interrogates her suspiciously, hilariously, about her writing—"'Are girls necessary?'"—the Biographer implies that "'a husband at the Cape,'" while hypocritical, perhaps, allows both Orlando and her lesbian poetry to elude moral surveillance.

The text's domestication of an imperialist national history into an individual sexual one recontains what the novel suggests are the revolutionary possibilities of lesbian desire: its challenges to English respectability and English notions of racial homogeneity, its contestation of gender roles, and its potential alliances with similarly "foreign" racial and sexual others. *Orlando*'s polymorphously perverse female subject can never be less than national; indeed, the last words of the novel— "Nineteen Hundred and Twenty-eight"—cite the year that universal suffrage granted the "superfluous woman" under thirty years of age full participation in the political processes of the nation, regardless of her marital status. In closing with the year in which England fully extended its notion of the voting citizen beyond the exclusions of gender and state-sanctioned sexuality, Woolf's text presents Orlando and the novel's readers with the task of renegotiating the sexual and racial terms of English national belonging. Contesting and adopting the identity constraints of nation and gender, *Orlando* slyly invites its readers to unmask the "joking" terms under which such femininity is produced—as gender identities are often, if not always, produced—as both a negotiation and subversion of the constraints of larger national, racial, and sexual inclusions.

UNDOMESTICATING SATIRE

Djuna Barnes's satire of Natalie Barney's Paris lesbian circle in *Ladies Almanack* undoes these domestications of lesbians and lesbian desire by undoing satire itself. Whereas satire usually occupies the distance between the narrator and its objects in order to comment upon them for readers who share the distanced narrator's point of view, *Ladies Almanack* reverses this process, and in the course of its narration undomesticates sexually perverse women by allowing the narrative point of view to collapse into the thickets of a wildly baroque prose style. Like her later novel *Nightwood,* where the distanced voice of the narrator becomes gradually displaced by the logorrheic monologues of the transvestite doctor Matthew O'Connor, *Ladies Almanack* is greatly taken up with the wisdom and exploits of a central sexually perverse character, in this case Dame Evangeline Musset. Unlike *Nightwood,* however, the narrator's diction and choice of images become indistinguishable from the voices of its characters, thus allowing the distanced satirical eye to give way, to bridge the distance between its point of view and that of the characters it supposedly fixes in its gaze. This operates not so much to domesticate the characters as it does to undomesticate and queer the satirical eye, which, instead of appropriating the look in order to normalize the characters it looks at, rather allows the queerness of the style of the characters, the aesthetic of their speech, to unsettle it, to narrow the distance between seer and seen, and dissolve the gazer and its objects of scrutiny into a sea of wild language.

The satiric voice blunts its own critique from the very beginning: "Now this be a Tale of as fine a Wench as ever wet Bed, she who was called Evangeline Musset and who was in her Heart one Grand Red Cross for the Pursuance, the Relief and the Distraction, of such Girls as in their Hinder Parts, and their Fore Parts, and in whatsoever Parts did suffer them most, lament Cruelly."[10] The humor of the satire lies in the reduction of women to their bodies, and to Dame Musset's own reduction of her subjectivity and intellect to addressing the needs of those bodies. Her sole purpose in life, we are told, is to alleviate sexual desire as it manifests itself in women's physical symptoms. Dame Musset is thus a kind of lesbian sexual apothecary or healer, one far less interested in the spiritual or poetic aspects of love than she is in its fleshly incarnations. With the description of Dame Musset's mistaken gender at birth, however, the text undoes its view of female bodies as innately comic and ridiculous. Dame Musset is, like Radclyffe Hall's lesbian heroine Stephen Gordon, a girl who should have been a boy, but "when therefore, she came forth an Inch or so less than this, she paid no Heed to the Error" (7). Now the satire turns from its scrutiny of women's bodies and desires to the absurdity that a mere "Inch" is all that distinguishes boys from girls. All distinctions that value one kind of body over another, or even differentiate one body from another, are ridiculous and unjust, since—as Dame Musset is quick to point out to her father when he criticizes her masculinity—any body can perform any gender, regardless of how many bits of flesh it possesses or lacks: "'Thou, good Governor, wast expecting a Son when you lay atop of your Choosing, why then be so mortal wounded when you perceive that you have your Wish? Am I not doing after your very Desire, and is it not the more commendable, seeing that I do it without the Tools for the Trade, and yet nothing complain?'" (8).

The next chapter further undercuts the notion of critical voice and critical distance when it introduces the much less understanding sensibility of Patience Scalpel: "Thus her Voice was heard throughout the Year, as cutting in its Derision as a surgical Instrument, nor did she use it to come to other than a Day and yet another Day in which she said, 'I have tried all means, Mathematical, Poetical, Statistical and Reasonable, to come to the Core of this Distemper, known as Girls! Girls!'" (12). Now the narrator actually criticizes the voice "cutting in its Derision" that criticizes lesbian desire. Patience Scalpel is satirized for her inability to understand the lesbians of her circle, and her limited point of view is the one being made fun of in the text. In contrast, Dame Musset has come to understand the entire world: "I have learned on the Bodies of all Women, all Customs, and from their Minds have all Nations given up their Secrets" (35). All writing and all talking exist for the sole purpose of seduction, and the narrative voice, in seeking to convey "what a woman says to a Woman and she be up to her Ears in Love's Acre" (42), launches into poetry, supposedly paraphrased from the lesbian discussed in the text, but aimed for the ears and eyes of readers:

> For you alone I reserve that Gasp under Gasp, that Sigh behind Sigh, that Attention back of feigned; that Cloud's Silver is yours—take it! What care I on whom it rains! The real me is your real yours, I can spend myself in Hedgerow and Counter-patch, 'tis only the Dust of my reality, the Smoke that tells of the Fire, which my own Darling Lamb, my most perfect and tirelessly different, is yours, I am thine! You compel me! (44–45)

At these moments the language rises beyond satire with a dignity and a fierce beauty, seizing its Blakean images and flinging them back defiantly in its extreme language of love, a language whose muscularity is plucked roots and all from the dark recesses of Elizabethan and Jacobean English prose. This address is breathtaking; this desire powerful, unassailable, the gushing of a natural force that turns aside humor with the power of its feeling. Patience Scalpel's "core of Distemper" is revealed in all its splendor as the ultimate surrender of body, spirit, and desire to the beloved, and in the deeply powerful language, the language of the King James Bible and Burton's *Anatomy of Melancholy*, that sounds the spiritual and creative depths of this surrender.

The point of view of Patience Scalpel is finally utterly discredited, first by the satiric narrative point of view, then by Dame Musset herself. The narrator's tone is quite funny here, calling attention to its own objectivity—"it is sadly against me to report"—while not refraining from giving damning opinions under the guise of such sympathy, suggesting that alcohol is responsible for Patience's mistaken faith in her own ability to please women sexually:

> Again, just as there are some Fellows who will brag that they can teach a Woman much and yet again, and be her all-in-one, there are, alike, Women, no wiser, who maintain that they could (had they a mind to) teach a taught Woman; thus though it is sadly against me to report it of one so curing to the Wound as Patience Scalpel, yet did she (on such Evenings as saw her facing her favorite Vintage, for no otherwise would she have brought herself to it,) hint, then aver, and finally boast that she herself, though all Thumbs at the business and an Amateur, never, having gone so much as a Nose-length into the Matter, could mean as much to a Woman as another, though the gentle purring of "Nay! Nay! Nay!" from the Furs surrounding Dame Musset continued to bleed in her Flank. (50)

The narrator slyly lets the readers know that Patience's ignorance of lesbian sexual practices is not shared by the narrator. Euphemistic in-jokes, such as being "all Thumbs," indicate clumsiness in its more generally understood sense, but also suggest Patience's mistaken overreliance on manual stimulation of a sexual partner, not to mention her indexterous use of the clumsiest and shortest digits on the hand while doing so, and her inexperience with cunnilingus, "never having gone so much as a Nose-length into the matter." Patience is boasting about things she knows nothing about, and the narrator, who knows quite a bit, is onto her.

The satiric point of view is thus a lesbian point of view; the "normal" frame of the satiric narrative relies not on a conventional view of women and sexuality, but instead establishes a sexually queer point of view as a valid frame. What this queer frame does, however, is reverse the terms of satire, establish the lesbian narrator and lesbian critic as the most reliable voice, and undomesticate and free up the sexually perverse lesbian by domesticating and satirizing the limited perspective of her supposedly socially preferable counterpart, the sexually "normal" woman. These lesbian satires constitute a specific kind of dynamic portraiture where the normal, normative look, the look of convention, or the look that is seen to demand conventional behavior, is perversely sent up. This alone is important in that it responds to the attempt on the part of normative satirists, such as Mackenzie and Lewis, to hijack the queer looking of modernist portraiture and reestablish the frame of the normal as the portraitist's frame of reference. However, in speaking to an "in" crowd of readers—or creating the illusion of an "in" crowd who understands the Bloomsburyish jokes in *Orlando,* or the personalities in *Ladies Almanack*—while taking care to speak to a larger audience, these lesbian satires invoke and produce a community. In this community, normativity can circulate as a joke that everybody agrees nobody believes in. As we shall see, not only normative ideals of behavior but even the norms of authentic identity itself can circulate in this way, producing portraits that interrogate the frames of portraiture and the assumptions of those who turn back to modernism looking for authentic persons, celebrities, and geniuses.

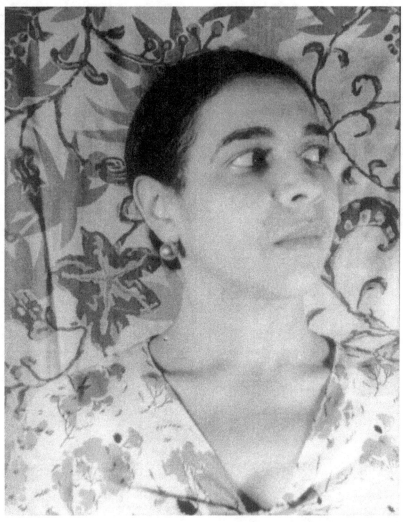

Nella Larsen photographed by Carl Van Vechten (1932). The Yale Collection of American Literature, Beinecke Rare Book Room and Manuscript Library. By permission of the Carl Van Vechten Trust.

4

FORGERY, OR, FAKING IT

In lesbian modernism, feminine masquerade is a variation on the framed self-elaboration that from Wilde onward operates as the central dynamic of modernist portraiture. Modernism's portraits of women uncovering a woman in the act of staging particular versions of herself suggest that many writers were intrigued with the idea of lesbian personae lurking beneath various everyday performances of heterosexual femininity. "Faking it" functions as part of feminine invention and self-invention in such modern texts as Colette's *The Pure and the Impure*, Marie Stope's treatise *Married Love*, Bourdet's Broadway play *The Captive*, Nella Larsen's *Passing*, Gertrude Stein's *Autobiography of Alice B. Toklas*, and even Ernest Hemingway's *A Moveable Feast*. Feminist critics have often read this theme as indicative of closeted or coded texts; Catharine Stimpson has famously described this as "the Lesbian lie" used by writers such as Gertrude Stein, whose "modulation of subversion into entertainment both follows and refines a homosexual method of seeking acceptance in modern heterosexual culture."[1]

Much has been written about *Alice B. Toklas* in the decades since Stimpson's assertion, and Stimpson's notion of the identity and sexual label "lesbian" as essential truth underneath the "lie" of self-invention clearly misses the sheer enjoyment of hearing one's self telling that is crucial to *Alice B. Toklas* and its contemporaneous sister texts. But Stimpson's critique also senses, if it misreads, the larger art of impersonation, of faking acceptable or conventional modes of femininity and feminine sexual responsiveness, circulating in this moment. Stein's sly self-invention—and that of her contemporaries—is a pleasurable impersonation that faking it dramatizes and circulates, the self-conscious reproduction of feminine artifice as a way of being modern, of doing modernity. "Faking it" stages the appropriation of the terms of feminine expression in this moment, operating as a framing and distancing device in much the same way that logorrheic chatter also emphasized the self-conscious playing of a role for many of modernism's male voices.

The writer Colette begins her extraordinary 1932 book of portraits of the Parisian sexual demimonde, *Ces Plaisirs,* published nine years later as *Le pur et l'impur,* with the study of Charlotte, a beautiful woman who makes a virtuoso performance out of faking orgasms. It is significant that Colette begins with "Charlotte," for "Charlotte" epitomizes the era's fascination with the queerness of feminine signification, with a feminine heterosexuality that only exists in masquerade, impersonation, and improvisation:

> But from the depths of this very silence a sound imperceptibly began in a woman's throat, at first husky, then clear, asserting its firmness and amplitude as it was repeated, becoming clear and full like the notes the nightingale repeats and accumulates until they pour out in a flood of arpeggios. . . . Up there on the balcony a woman was trying hard to delay her pleasure and in doing so was hurrying it toward its climax and destruction, in a rhythm at first so calm and harmonious, so marked that I involuntarily beat time with my head, for its cadence was as perfect as its melody.
>
> My unknown neighbor half sat up and muttered to himself, "That's Charlotte."[2]

Charlotte's performance of sexual pleasure as sexual style narrates heterosexuality as a joyous and uncomplicated inevitability for women, one where they find their happiness in the public display of themselves as alluring, sexually confident, and feminine. She impresses the narrator because her measured cries represent a unity between body and expression, a "calm and harmonious" and "perfect" relation that is striking because it seems to epitomize ideal, "normal" female sexual response. And yet what ultimately proves most remarkable about Charlotte's melody—and the narrator's response to it—is not its truth but its remarkable falseness.

In a later conversation with Charlotte, the narrator "realizes" that it is all an act, though the reader who remembers that the narrator "involuntarily" beat time to Charlotte's faked orgasm might suspect the narrator herself of feigned belief in the realness of Charlotte's pleasure. Suddenly loving a man is not woman's pleasure and gratification, but an effort, a performance, an artifice. At this very moment, the moment of artifice, Charlotte offers the narrator the secret of feminine interiority, not as proof of the "normal" matchup of feminine display and inner feminine pleasure, but femininity as surface and style, of style as surface only, of personality and interiority as the *performance* of depth rather than proof of "true" deep essence. Another version of Oscar Wilde's portrait-within-a-portrait, *The Picture of Dorian Gray,* Charlotte opens this book of modernist portraits with the revelation of feminist performance as a lie, as faking it, as impersonation. In this instance it becomes possible to see modernisms giving way to style in expression, style in character, style in the joy of performing personalities, and relinquishing fictions of deep character, essence, interiority, individuality, and realism. The inspirational effect Charlotte has on the narrator testifies to the narrator's recognition of Charlotte's art as revolutionary:

> This substantial Charlotte was a female genius, indulging in tender subterfuge, consideration, and self-denial. And here she was, this woman who knew how to reassure men, sitting beside me, limbs relaxed, idly waiting to take up again the duty of one who loves best: the daily imposture, the deferential lie, the passionately maintained dupery, the unrecognized feat of valor that expects no reward. . . . Our concealed identity and accidental proximity, the surrounding atmosphere of so-called debauchery were alone what had loosened the tongue of this heroine whose silence in no way embarrassed me, this stranger to whom I told nothing, as though I had finished telling her all I had to tell. (18)

At this point in the description, Charlotte is "substantial" and "a female genius" whose art is in pleasing others rather than herself, whose "identity" is a shifting secret, whose heroism is unknown. Charlotte's "substance" is not real essence but performance, an interiority only revealed as artifice by artifice. The narrator is attracted to this Charlotte, acutely aware of her physical presence, of the placement and proximity of her limbs, and this attraction motivates the narrator to reveal her own queer desires, desires directed toward women and men, engendered and inspired by an aesthetics of lying. In faking it, Charlotte reveals herself as a genius, not to mention a lesbian muse, and the narrator herself, who may also have been faking it, is given license to rhapsodize about the exteriorized production of female "interiority" as an important site of art.

Charlotte's art inspires the narrator's own stream-of-consciousness images, images where different women she has been and known are battered by their own gendered flesh: "Her presence lured other ephemera from the depths of my memory, phantoms I seem always to be losing and finding again, restless ghosts unrecovered from wounds sustained in the past when they crashed headlong or sidelong against that barrier reef, mysterious and comprehensible, the human body" (18–19). In revealing the supposed "depth" of her pleasure as mere surface art, Charlotte gestures to a secret self whose presence is only indicated through this complicated performance of deep surface. Images of women as endangered swimmers torn against the reefs of their own bodies suggest gender as both a death and a magical transformation, one where physical sex has no authentic relation to gendered and sexual personae, but where sexual attraction calls forth "ephemera" and "ghosts unrecovered," transforming and bringing forth many selves.

"Faking it" is an important lesbian modernist style, one that stages the woman genius as a confounding, mixed, shifting combination of signifier and signified, artist and object, genius and muse. "Charlotte" revealed as mask, as chivalrous femme, as the signified of man's desire, is also Charlotte as genius, as artist, as signifier, as alarming paper tiger. Colette's portrait of herself uncovering the woman staging herself as a particular version of "Charlotte" revels in the layering of personae in the performance of heterosexual femininity. One feels the sheer enjoyment of penetration, duplicity, and impersonation reading that voice, as it moves in and out of the consciousnesses of its characters and its narrator in turn. Its lesbianism lies not in its truth as "real" essence underneath the masquerade, but in this spectacle of the voice taking narrative pleasure in itself.

WOMEN IMPERSONATE WOMEN

In *Married Love*, her 1918 polemic advocating birth control and marriage reform, Dr. Marie Stopes addressed the theme of faking sexual pleasure, condemning it by comparing it to the sham orgasms of prostitutes. Stopes's analysis of "bought love" as a carefully fashioned, if misleading, commodity blamed prostitutes for misleading men about their sexual prowess, which she saw as the reason for the tendency on the part of many men to blame their wives for frigidity rather than look to their own sexual technique as requiring improvement. In the "passing" prostitute in Stopes one sees the figure of the woman who fakes it, here positioned outside of marriage, but operating already as a threat to marital happiness because of her misleading sexual duplicity:

They [husbands] argue that, because the prostitute showed physical excitement and pleasure in union, if the bride or wife does not do so, then she is "cold" or "undersexed." They may not realize that often all the bodily movements which the prostitute makes are studied and simulated because her client enjoys his climax best when the woman in his arms simultaneously thrills.[3]

A decade later, this faking woman became the full-blown "lesbian threat" of the twenties and thirties, against which companionate heterosexuality solidified its identity as authentic, normal, and healthy by helping to establish the era's link between lesbianism, duplicity, and impersonation.[4]

In one of the more famous psychoanalytic portraits depicting faking it in the modernist era, and the one that has proven most useful for postmodern critical studies of theatrical self-presentation and strategic identity—Joan Riviere's 1929 case study, "Womanliness as a Masquerade"—faking it completely undoes the authenticity of heterosexual femininity and female sexual response by suggesting that femininity and enthusiastic feminine heterosexual performance is a way of being a masculine-identified lesbian.[5] Riviere's study helped form Judith Butler's notion of gender as performative rather than essential in *Gender Trouble* and *Bodies That Matter*, but Butler's work picks up on the anxiety of Riviere's masquerading women to stress the compulsive aspects of all gender performativity, rather than emphasize the pleasurable, powerful, and creative modes of femininity one finds in twentieth-century writers like Colette. One of the first translators of Freud's works into English,[6] Riviere argues that masquerading women are not passing, or veiling their "true" identities beneath the strain of a role at wild variance with who they really are, but are expressing something crucial about gendered comportment and the representation of interiority as style in modernity. Femininity, at least in its exaggerated and theatrical mode, *is* a queer expression where the gaze can be solicited and resisted at the same time, one whose lesbianism and masculine identification enables a perverse mobility that is both outside and within conventional identities.

Riviere's study appears to discuss several different women, but uses all of them to sketch a general type of woman, or a portrait of femininity as and through its performers. Her chief subject suffers from acute anxiety that men will not like her, and thus she seems at first an unlikely candidate to look at in order to understand the pleasure of performance. However, in the case of the masquerade, since male approval is the measure of her successful performance, and thus one of the main avenues for her self-enjoyment, her pleasure is something she finds afterward, in their esteem and attentiveness toward her. Another woman in Riviere's study similarly finds pleasure in the very tension her activities seem destined to resolve. This woman actually uses heterosexuality, and her enjoyment of her own performance of heterosexuality, in order to be more masculine, to have frequent orgasms, and to compete with men in the realm of pleasure *as* a man: "She was afraid of impotence in exactly the same way as a man . . . on deeper levels it was a determination not to be beaten by the man."[7] Another version of Colette's Charlotte, this woman is acutely self-conscious, aware of being looked at, measured and found wanting, so she performs normalcy with a vengeance, turning the drama of her own castration or "impotence" into a pleasure, a triumph in the "realm of pleasure" she is not supposed to rule but does. Other women in Riviere's study enjoy the castrating power white femininity allows them to exercise over working-class and African American men—a power they can always disavow by appealing to white male chivalry and racism.

Reading Riviere's masquerade through Lacan's theory of mimicry (itself derived from modernist insights about biology) emphasizes "faking it" as a subversive and dynamic act of consciousness and self-consciousness, one linked in modernism to lesbianism and therefore one whose lesbianism performs its own distance and approximation of heterosexual norms. Jacques Lacan addresses "faking it" in his discussion of coloration mimicry, where he defines its compulsory imitation as "simply a way of defending oneself against light." According to this interpretation, then, mimicry is a defense against being seen that works by giving the look something to look at—but something different from the "real" self of the mimic. Robert Samuels elaborates on Lacan's reading, suggesting that "It is, in fact, this presence of the gaze that causes the inversion of the subject's consciousness and narcissism."[8] For Samuels, being looked at results in a self-consciousness linked to narcissism, in a seeing one's self that takes refuge in the self-absorption of display. But Lacan also gives the creature who mimics the power to solicit the gaze, to give something to be looked at by impersonating the place of being looked at. Lacan calls this place the "stain" (99). The act of mimicry dramatizes the subject's being seen, and the stain becomes the representation of the gaze.

Thus the mimic marks the place where self-consciousness makes it possible to look back, satirize, solicit, and torque the gaze. Ellie Ragland argues that this gaze, this stain, this "Something given to be seen" is also "something which Lacan equates with the *awareness* of consciousness"(original italics). In other words, mimicry dramatizes self-consciousness, which in turn dramatizes the incoherence of identity and the "I": "This awareness is like daylight that startles one on awaking in a strange bed, unsure for a moment of what constitutes 'I' as an identity."[9] Mimicry—faking it—does this in systems that offer the illusion of coherent consciousness, of unified identity and coherent selves where outer surface reflects inner depth, as part of ideologies intent on establishing and maintaining behavioral norms. Heterosexuality marked by conventional gender is one such system. Lesbian duplicity dramatizes the illusory coherence of heterosexual norms and undermines their authenticity by showing that anyone can fake them.

CAPTIVE WIVES

The theme of "faking it" in drama and fiction of the era similarly championed heterosexual enthusiasm and served to critique it, often at the same time. In 1926, for example, faking it as heterosexual passing took center stage in the highly controversial American production of Edouard Bourdet's play *La Prisonnière*, or *The Captive*, which ran for five months on Broadway before being shut down by the Manhattan district attorney's office. Taking its title from a volume of Proust's *À la recherche du temps perdu* where the narrator lives in his mother's apartment with his bisexual lover Albertine, Bourdet's *The Captive* combines the wartime paranoia engendered by the Mata Hari spy scandal with the postwar interest in companionate marriage. The story of the play revolves around a young woman named Irene who pretends to be in love with her childhood male friend, Jacques, in order to escape her father's surveillance. In the course of the play Irene convinces Jacques, who has always loved her, to marry her in order to save her from her lesbianism. Unable even to imagine that two women might love each other sexually, the innocent, chivalrous Jacques gradually uncovers the truth of Irene's passion for a married women. In one of the play's many melodramatic monologues on the evils of lesbianism, Jacques is warned by the woman's husband not to get mixed up with sexually deviant women:

> Friendship, yes—that's the mask. Under cover of friendship a woman can enter any household, whenever and however she pleases—at any hour of the day—she can poison and pillage everything before the man whose home she destroys is even aware of what's happening to him.

When finally he realizes things it's too late—he is alone! Alone in the
face of a secret alliance of two beings who understand one another
because they're alike, because they're of the same sex, because they're of
a different planet than he, the stranger, the enemy![10]

Here lesbianism wreaks its havoc on the heterosexual home—and,
the language implies, the heterosexual race—by virtue of its hidden-
ness and secrecy, through the ability of the lesbian to pass disguised as
respectable and heterosexually feminine. Her sexual espionage is fur-
thered by the ignorance of those who cannot recognize her. What is
most interesting, however, is the acknowledgment of the power of the
woman who fakes heterosexuality. She and her lesbian companions
are capable of warlike destruction; their dangerous alliances pose
more of a threat to bourgeois heterosexual civilization than any mili-
tary power.

The Captive is a profoundly heterosexual play, in that it is a drama
interested in undoing social performance and style as libidinal pleasures, substituting the "realer" pleasures of the body, sincerity, and
sexual responsiveness for those of the aesthetic realm. This agenda suggests the extent to which passing, impersonation, and performance
were considered queer, perverse, and dangerous. Moreover, Irene's
physical response to the violets her lover sends her, which come to stand
for the woman who is always offstage, and which leave her, in Jacques's
disgusted opinion, "breathless," "dazed," and "trembling," defines lesbian desire in the play as an elsewhere, an aesthetic, sensuous, and sentimental realm that touches the senses but is not embodied, or necessarily physical. This aesthetic and imaginative realm is further
suggested by Irene's horrified dismissal of heterosexual sex: "I expected
a little more tenderness. Is there no spirit in love? Must it be only—*the
body!*" (251; original italics).

The play implies that the benefits of faking it for lesbians are husband, home, and social respectability. Yet in the end Irene has none of
these. Irene leaves Jacques when her lover, Madame d'Augines, shows
up at Irene's favorite painting gallery to beg for her, while Jacques
returns to Françoise, the mistress he had previously dumped. In this
Jacques seems to have it all, while Irene and her mysterious lover must
wander Europe as homeless, husbandless exiles. At the end of the play,
however, when both he and Irene go out at different moments, his exit
will take him merely to another room, another body, and another
domestic scene with different characters, much like the one he has left.
Irene, whose lover importunes her with violets and pursues her through

the avenues of art, sentiment, and the senses, will escape into the world, into the emotions, and into imaginative realms.

The Captive often seems to perversely forget, or repress, its status as a play. It clearly means to resolve its story with the climax of Irene's revelation that she is still in love with Madame d'Augines, a climax that leads Jacques to return to his mistress Françoise with renewed appreciation for her heterosexual responsiveness to his caress: *"Their lips meet. She abandons herself to him. The kiss, a long one, leaves her prostrated, her head thrown back on his shoulder, her eyes closed"* (232; original italics). These hilariously overwrought stage directions seem designed to demonstrate that his lover is a real woman, and to convince audiences that he is right to seek happiness in her arms and divorce his lesbian wife. Yet anyone seeing the play might also wonder if its resolution is really a resolution at all, or whether Françoise, having gotten her revenge on Jacques for throwing her over, is really going to abandon her flapper's ways to settle down with him. How can an audience tell if Françoise's "real" response to Jacques's kiss is any truer than Irene's pathetic wifely compliances? What can we make of our sense when we read this play that this scene would be immensely fun to do? Françoise's pleasure here—and that of the actress we hypothesize to have enjoyed herself playing this part—may also be, like Charlotte's, the pleasure of the actress, the pleasure of duplicity, of faking it, impersonation, masquerade, and passing. This kind of pleasure is the pleasure of artifice somewhere between lesbianism and heterosexuality, partial to both. This pleasure opens the door to reading female theatricality as a lesbian aesthetic, one strengthened by the fact that when we find its self-conscious art in modernist portraiture, it is usually hugely enjoying itself.

At least one writer who either saw or heard about the play may have read Françoise's performance with skepticism. Several years after *The Captive* appeared in Europe and then on Broadway, another Irene appears in a slim novel by Nella Larsen, then a young librarian living in Harlem. The photographic portraits of Larsen by her friend Carl Van Vechten show his interest in Larsen, an uneasy-looking woman posed against patterned backgrounds, as an element in some larger design. Since Van Vechten was one of the white patrons who enthusiastically championed Harlem writers and artists as "primitive" voices, his posing Larsen against such designs, her strained expression in these portraits, and the themes she took up in her writing all show her struggle as an African American artist to work within the frame of primitivism and break out of it at the same time.

Since its editing and reissue by Deborah McDowell in 1986, Nella

Larsen's 1929 novel *Passing* has garnered a heavy volume of critical attention. McDowell's reading of lesbian desire as the text's central subtext remains the dominant interpretation of the novel, one where racial passing and sexual passing become articulated as the dilemma of African American femininity. *Passing* centers on the tragedy of an upper-middle-class African American woman trapped in the masquerades of marriage, where women fake their sexual and racial identities in order to be safe and secure; McDowell's reading, which acknowledges the double bind faced by African American women seeking sexual freedom while also trying to shed a cultural image of "primitive" sexual licentiousness, also relies on post–sexual revolution assumptions about the liberatory aspect of free sexual expression.

According to this reading, lesbian desire operates in the novel as a metaphor for the sexual freedom the central character cannot allow herself to enjoy because she must uphold the appearance of sexual respectability as an emblem of race pride. Lesbianism to Irene is not merely a sexuality among other sexualities, but sexuality itself, one whose indulgence appears to her as a dangerous and selfish act. But *Passing* is about the pleasures of racial, sexual, class, and gender passing as well, and therein lies its affinity with modernist impersonation and improvisation more generally. Although Irene disapproves of these pleasures, she nevertheless engages in them and ultimately embraces them herself by the end of the novel. Sexually reticent and socially proper, Irene is nevertheless drawn to the exuberant finesse of her passing friend Clare's performance of whiteness and femininity, to her ability to impersonate heterosexual feminine ideals of flirtatiousness and "fake it," while enjoying her own performance immensely: "Clare had a trick of sliding down ivory lids over astonishing black eyes and then lifting them suddenly and turning on a caressing smile. Men like Dave Freeland fell for it. And Brian."[11] Indeed, although Irene's reserved, modest style of dress and comportment seems to reflect someone who flees the look rather than solicits it, Clare's embodiment of feminine performance *as* performance makes Irene all too aware of her own strenuous efforts to fake it, to be the proper Harlem socialite, to simulate marital concord in a relationship that has degenerated into cold formality. *Passing*'s take on the pleasures of impersonation, masquerade, and faking it extends Riviere's conclusions about the strategic nature of gender identity to racial identity as well, and makes race a style and a performance as well as an identification.

At certain moments, when Irene is most aware of her own artificiality, her misery is reflected as a kind of suffering self-consciousness, one that nevertheless takes pleasure in its own courage and secrecy: "In the second she saw that she could bear anything, but only if no one knew that she had anything to bear. It hurt. It frightened her, but she could bear it" (221). Irene begins to fashion her own masquerade of innocence quite deliberately and self-consciously in order to safeguard her dignity and her security, and this shifts the balance of power in the novel away from Clare and toward herself. The tragedy of Irene's self-consciousness is that she denies the very real pleasure she takes in artifice—her own and Clare's—and in her fantasies of self-denial and sacrifice. When Clare's double life is revealed, leaving her possibly free to take up with Irene's husband, Irene pushes Clare from a window to her death, and she decides to pass for heterosexually responsive. Irene faints at the end, sinking down into an unconscious "darkness," but she also sinks out of sight, unobserved and undetected in the double life she has chosen. Her lack of conviction in the truth of identity, a loss reflected in her strategic decision to embrace the fictions of heterosexual feminine and racial authenticity strategically, allows her to survive, while Clare, who believes in authenticity enough to give up passing, is snuffed out.

A WIFE HAS A GENIUS

Not only do *The Captive, Passing,* and Riviere's theory of feminine masquerade stage heterosexual femininity and lesbianism as indistinguishable from each other, but they also help position the two main literary portraits of late modernism and its aftermath—Gertrude Stein's *Autobiography of Alice B. Toklas* and Hemingway's *A Moveable Feast*—as part of a lesbian modernism that uses portraiture and impersonation to queer writing and history. Like many of the portraits of the modernist era, Stein's *Autobiography of Alice B. Toklas* is a portrait within a portrait. In this case, the framing portrait is that of Alice B. Toklas, supposedly drawn by herself but—as readers are constantly reminded—actually drawn by Stein. The portrait of Alice, then, is actually a portrait of Alice drawing portraits of the people she has known as a result of her long association with Stein. Like many of the modernist portraits discussed earlier, this portrait or series of portraits within a portrait allows the text to play with the dynamic relation between artist and subject, interiority and milieu, and life and art.

Critics have debated the meaning of Stein's impersonation in the *Autobiography;* some have read it as a buoyant but coded lesbian text, conservative in its heterosexual "packaging" of lesbianism but innovative in the ways it undermines the notion of a "core subject" whose narrator and subject are one and the same.[12] Others have emphasized this innovation, pointing out how it creates an "intimate" group of readers who share the narrator's pleasure in telling stories.[13] I want to take up this thread that emphasizes the narrative pleasure of the text in order to show how much of this pleasure is produced by impersonation. The pleasure here is not a by-product of textual encoding or even textual experimentation. Rather, the pleasure of the text *is* the meaning of text itself.

In *The Autobiography of Alice B. Toklas*, Gertrude Stein does not fake heterosexual femininity—as do her masquerading contemporaries and their characters—either sexually or in terms of identity. However, she does impersonate Alice B. Toklas, her wife, lover, and companion, and thus she fakes being a wife, but a very different kind of wife, inverting the terms of feminine masquerade so that they reveal the lesbian and her disguises, or rather, *as* her disguises. The wife Stein impersonates as "Alice" is a lesbian wife, the wife of a genius. Indeed, the first thing that the impersonation of Alice B. Toklas in Stein's *Autobiography of Alice B. Toklas* does is to produce a structure in which Stein can have Toklas designate her as a genius: "I was impressed by the coral brooch she wore and by her voice," "Alice" relates. "I may say that only three times in my life have I met a genius and each time a bell within me rang and I was not mistaken, and I may say in each case it was before there was any general recognition of the quality of genius in them" (660–61). "Alice" then goes on to list her three geniuses as Gertrude Stein, Pablo Picasso, and Alfred North Whitehead, but she only does so after "proving" her ability to recognize genius by insisting on the existence of a time before such genius was recognized by everybody.

The obvious problem of "Alice"'s reliability, given the context of impersonation where the author is using a character to praise herself, is resolved by a constant recourse to temporality, a recourse that helps establish "Alice" as a person who remembers things accurately. "Alice"'s validity as a speaker, in other words, is established through temporality, or rather through a temporal shift that helps establish the truth of her observations. The effect of this temporal shift is to call attention to the process of telling, rendering, and remembering. In the very moment of establishing "Alice" as a real teller, this shift paradoxically reminds readers that Stein is really telling the story. This temporal shift appears throughout the *Autobiography*, and it is similarly used to establish "Alice"'s narrative reliability at moments especially concerned with establishing the stature of Stein as a genius among her peers and contemporaries.

The second thing impersonation does in the *Autobiography* is to allow Stein to have Alice designate herself as Stein's wife. "The geniuses came and talked to Gertrude Stein and the wives sat with me" (748), "Alice" says, suggesting her own similar position as a wife. Earlier in the *Autobiography*, however, she does something different, something that, along with the nature of the impersonation of Alice that structures the book, problematizes her status as a wife rather than establishes it:

> Before I decided to write this book my twenty-five years with Gertrude
> Stein, I had often said that I would write, The wives of geniuses I have
> sat with. I have sat with so many. I have sat with wives who were not
> wives, of geniuses who were not real geniuses. I have sat with real wives
> of geniuses who were not real geniuses. I have sat with wives of
> geniuses, of near geniuses, of would be geniuses, in short I have sat very
> often and very long with many wives and wives of many geniuses. (671)

Here the pleasure of impersonation and the pleasure of remembering become the same thing. "Alice" enjoys running through the list of geniuses who were not geniuses, wives who were not wives, and all the possible combinations of these terms. This particular rendering of remembering seems to establish "Alice" as a person enjoying her memory of other people's impersonations of being a wife or being a genius. Telling becomes an exercise in combination and recombination that stresses improvisation and the fun of telling over historical accuracy. "Alice" is enjoying the combination of fiction and fact that is storytelling, and Stein is enjoying "Alice" enjoying herself. The pleasure of impersonation is multiple and layered here, but who is who? After all, we know these are not really geniuses, because "Alice" has met only three, but we also know that "Alice" isn't really Alice B. Toklas, but Stein impersonating Alice B. Toklas, so the reliability of "Alice"'s ability to distinguish genius is in doubt here. If "Alice" cannot recognize genius, then Stein is not a genius, and then neither can "Alice" be a wife. However, we know "Alice" is not really Stein's wife, because Stein is "Alice." Thus the question of who is really a wife and who a genius is as playfully indeterminate as a result of impersonation as it is in "Alice"'s story.

Unreliable identity is one of the chief pleasures of "faking it" that the text offers readers. Impersonation alone would designate the product of Stein's fake identity as Alice as a lesbian erotic collaboration, at least in fantasy. But the extended nature of Stein's impersonation, its series of portraits and reminiscences of real people, places, and events, does more than merely create a public statement of their relationship as one among the pantheon of modernist artistic and literary couples in Paris at the time.[14] It constitutes a way of writing that uses feminine masquerade—and the masculine-identified lesbianism associated with it—as a dynamic literary aesthetic. The pleasure of the narrator—and the narrator often seems to be enjoying herself immensely—is the pleasure "Stein" gives "Alice," and the pleasure "Stein" has being "Alice" is also the pleasure of "Alice" giving pleasure to herself as she remembers, renders, and seems to correct her story.

One story "Alice" recounts with seeming fondness is the story of Gertude Stein and her brother Leo buying their first Cézanne from the dealer Vollard. "Alice" creates and breaks the temporal and subjective frames of the story several times before she even arrives at the story, by leaping forward to tell what happened later in Stein's writing as a result of the visit:

> There were Cézannes to be seen at Vollard's. Later on Gertrude Stein wrote a poem called Vollard and Cézanne, and Henry McBride printed it in the New York Sun. This was the first fugitive piece of Gertrude Stein's to be so printed and it gave both her and Vollard a great deal of pleasure. Later on when Vollard wrote his book about Cézanne, Vollard at Gertrude Stein's suggestion sent a copy of the book to Henry McBride. She told Vollard that a whole page of one of New York's big daily papers would be devoted to his book. He did not believe it possible, nothing like that had ever happened to any body in Paris. It did happen and he was deeply moved and unspeakably content. But to return to that first visit. (687)

This is a rather wonderful performance of pretending to remember as someone else. Two sentences, one a little after the other, that begin with "later on" form a chain into the future that anchors this relationship between Vollard and Stein as mutually beneficial to both their arts. The relationship with Vollard gives Stein a poem, and the relationship with Stein gives Vollard both publicity as Stein's friend and art dealer, and a publisher for his book. The chain of events, recounted with seeming innocence by "Alice," serves to position Stein at the center of her circle and to make her a figure of success who in turn generously helps make her friends successful. Even more importantly, it creates a chain of literary successes for Stein and friends that actually eclipses the fact of Cézanne's paintings as the reason for their meeting in the first place. "Alice"'s memory helps replace modern painting—Cézanne—with modern literature—Stein—as the governing sensibility of the Paris avant-garde.

The story goes on to stress further that impersonation and imagination are more important than the paintings themselves. Gertrude and Leo ask Vollard for paintings by Cézanne; he goes upstairs and, after a long period of time, reappears with various strange paintings for them to examine; they ask for others, he goes upstairs, and the whole looking, talking, and waiting ritual commences again:

> By this time the early winter evening of Paris was closing in and just at this moment a very aged charwoman came down the same back stairs, mumbled, bon soir monsieur et madame, and quietly went out of the door, after a moment another old charwoman came down the same stairs, murmured, bon soir messieurs et mesdames and went quietly out of the door. Gertrude Stein began to laugh and said to her brother, it is all nonsense, there is no Cézanne. Vollard goes upstairs and tells these old women what to paint and he does not understand us and they do not understand him and they paint something and he brings it down and it is a Cézanne. They both began to laugh uncontrollably. (687–88)

"Alice" establishes the story temporally—"By this time," "after a moment"—in order to unravel "Cézanne" as an identity one might use to anchor a work of art. The fabrication of the story of there being no Cézanne, the suggestion that two charwomen might be the unwitting agents behind a major artistic cultural phenomenon, the assertion that art might be produced through comic misunderstanding, ignorance, and the desire to make a buck rather than as some manifestation of artistic genius—all of these are vastly more amusing conjectures than the actual story of Cézanne himself, or the fact of his paintings, or the history of their circulation, fame, and sales. In this way "Cézanne," like "Alice" and "Gertrude," becomes a creation of the text, or in this case, a creation of a creation ("Alice") of the text. The invention of Cézanne takes precedence over any historical Cézanne, and this "Cézanne" is vastly more amusing to the narrator, and thus to readers as well.

The style of the narrative has the simple words and simple sentences one associates with Stein's writing. The narrator affects simplicity also, but whereas Stein's narrators are often repetitious, with only a limited, sometimes rudimentary, understanding of their subjects and audiences, "Alice" has an endearing fondness for the characters she knows, even while they sometimes exasperate her, as well as a desire to please, to be fair, to remember people and events accurately. This "Alice" has a voice that one grows fond of in turn, that one misses when one stops reading—a friendly voice at one's elbow that seems to lack affectation and self-consciousness, an amiable voice of a storyteller asked to entertain a group of friends who responds good-naturedly but humbly, effacing her personality, or seeming to efface it, in the interests of the subject matter. What "Alice" enables Stein to do is to establish the validity of the surface, and the validity of narrating character as surface. Once surface validity in the present has been established, Stein can go back and render history as "Alice" in such a way as to render her own character as she wanted it understood.

For example, having established her voice in the present in the first three chapters, "Alice" backtracks in chapter 4 to "Gertrude Stein Before she came to Paris." Here the layers of impersonation become ever thicker, as Stein now impersonates Alice telling about Stein before she knew her—a self-portrait disguised as someone else's rendition of her history. This allows Stein to fashion herself as a genius, but a genius of all surface and no depth. "She understands very well the basis of creation and therefore her advice and criticism is invaluable to all her friends," "Alice" relates. "How often have I heard Picasso say to her when she has said something about a picture of his and then illustrated by something she was trying to do, *racontez-moi cela*. In other words tell me about it" (738). On the next page we are told "Gertrude Stein never had subconscious reactions, nor was she a successful subject for automatic writing" (739). This would seem to counter the model of genius as profound interiority. Instead, Stein wants herself to become like a painting, a portrait of all surfaces and style, and "Alice" helps her do this. The question is, why fashion yourself this way? Where does it get you? Why use "Alice" to do it?

One answer may lie in Stein's preference for obtuse or innocent narrators, also voices of surface, seemingly without interiority, as in her *Three Lives*. "Alice" is a matter-of-fact narrative persona, one without much reflection, who asserts that Stein has no interiority. This doubled lack of interiority, this impersonation of interiorlessness asserting interiorlessness, actually marks the opposite polarity of portrait painting from Wilde's *The Picture of Dorian Gray*, with its portrait of a portrait that becomes all depth of character, so much so that its surface is marred and its subject unrecognizable. In spite of the play of surfaces Dorian's friend Lord Henry celebrates in the novel, it always dissolves into narcissism, interiority, self-absorption. Stein's distancing mechanisms have the reverse effect; there is no interiority in Stein, or "Alice," in the *Autobiography*, though it is no less pleasurable as a result of this.

The result is an artfully guileless narrative, one whose innocence and surface sincerity can never be read as authentic, since we know it is impersonation to begin with. It can only be read as the impersonation of authenticity, sincerity, and identity, and this is a large part of its delightfulness, as well as its delight in itself. One of the best examples of this affectation of nonaffectation, and the pleasure of narration that this impersonation brings, is in the famous story of Picasso's on-again, off-again lover Fernande's party, where "Alice" calls attention several times to herself telling the story:

> Everybody sat down and everybody began to eat rice and other things, that is as soon as Guillaume Apollinaire and Rousseau came in which they did very presently and were wildly acclaimed. How well I remember their coming, Rousseau a little small colourless frenchman with a little beard, like any number of frenchmen one saw everywhere. Guillaume Apollinaire with finely cut florid features, dark hair and a beautiful complexion. (769)

The hilarity escalates from here, with portraits of the way people look being replaced by descriptions of the way people behave, sometimes wildly, the more they have to drink. What is striking is the movement in the narration between the particular that seems to support an assertion of the truth of a located narrator we can trust, on the one hand, and the messy diachronicity that more closely resembles the way people really tell stories, sometimes skipping over physical descriptions and large chunks of time, sometimes relishing minute details of how people look and what they say and do, backtracking and skipping ahead. "How well I remember their coming," the narrator "Alice" asserts, then again she corrects herself with an "Oh, yes," and finally brings both together in a phrase that gestures toward chronological accuracy while muddling it: "Then a little later":

> At the sight of Guillaume, Marie who had become comparatively calm seated next to Gertrude Stein, broke out again in wild movements and outcries. Guillaume got her out of the door and downstairs and after a decent interval they came back Marie a little bruised but sober. By this time everybody had eaten everything and poetry began. Oh, yes, before this Frederic of the Lapin Agile and the University of Apaches had wandered in with his usual companion a donkey, was given a drink and wandered out again. Then a little later some italian street singers hearing of the party came in. Fernande rose at the end of the table and

flushed and her forefinger straight into the air said it was not that kind
of party, and they were promptly thrown out. (769–70)

Again we have the reminder of the teller telling, the corrections and
backtracking that create the fiction of a persona creating a narrative
from memory for an audience. But by now the voice is both Gertrude
and Alice, one that deeply enjoys emphasizing its own feats of impersonation, characterization, remembering, and narrating. This blended
voice insists on its own artifice over and over, yet also allows the pleasure of character, in this case the invented amalgamated "Alice," to
emerge as a self-conscious portrait, a portrait that always insists on its
own status as a portrait. "Faking it" in *The Autobiography of Alice B. Toklas*
holds sitter and artist in constant tension, exchanging each with the
other so that the object that is made between them undoes any difference between genius and wife, lesbian and woman, speaker and character, history and fiction, essence and impersonation. "Faking it" makes
a style out of the seeming refusal of style, a depth out of the refusal to be
anything but surface, a wife out of a genius and a genius out of a wife,
an artist out of the subject and a subject out of the artist.

The temporal reversals that characterize memory and telling in the
Autobiography extend, finally, to portraiture itself, a description of which
only occurs near the end of this portrait of a woman drawing portraits.
In a passage that ends with "This was the beginning of the long series of
portraits. She has written portraits of practically everybody she has
known, and written them in all manners and in all styles" (777), Stein-
as-Toklas narrates the beginning of Stein's foray into literary portraiture.
She does this by showing Alice's reaction to an earlier portrait of her:

> Helene used to stay at home with her husband Sunday evening, that is
> to say she was always willing to come but we often told her not to
> bother. I like cooking, I am an extremely good five-minute cook, and
> beside [*sic*], Gertrude Stein liked from time to time to have me make
> american dishes. One Sunday evening I was very busy preparing one of
> these and then I called Gertrude Stein to come in from the atelier for
> supper. She came in much excited and would not sit down. Here I want
> to show you something, she said. No I said it has to be eaten hot. No, she
> said, you have to see this first. (776–77)

This is one of the only conversations between "Gertrude" and "Alice" in
the text. It is striking for its brief dip into their subjective depths and
domestic preferences—we find out something intimate about each of

their likes and dislikes, we find out that this is a source of tension around mealtimes, we find out that Alice is an extremely good five-minute cook. In this portrait of the beginning of Stein's portraits we are given a portrait of them together, a portrait of their domesticity that frames and contextualizes all the other portraits in the text, including that of Alice: "I thought she was making fun of me and I protested, she says I protest now about my autobiography." Again we have the temporal shifts, again we are reminded that we are witnessing an impersonation. Stein's mimicry of Alice, her mimicry of herself, and her playful rendering of the two of them at dinner dramatizes the incoherence of identity, the making coherent of identity through representation, impersonation, collaboration, desire:

> Gertrude Stein never likes her food hot and I do like mine hot, we never agree about this. She admits that one can wait to cool it but one cannot heat it once it is on a plate so it is agreed that I have it served as hot as I like. In spite of my protests and the food cooling I had to read. I can still see the little tiny pages of the note-book written forward and back. It was the portrait called Ada, the first in Geography and Plays. I began it and I thought she was making fun of me and I protested, she says I protest now about my autobiography. Finally I read it all and was terribly pleased with it. And then we ate our supper. (777)

Instead of a coherent identity, voice, and history we have a coherent voice intent on undermining the basis of its coherence on every front. Their lesbian duplicity—are they wives, geniuses, neither, both? Are they women? Are they fact or fiction? One voice or two?—exposes the illusory coherence of norms, of character, depth, interiority, history, while circulating the gleeful pleasures that "faking it" affords its sly actresses.

A HUNGRY HEART

Years after the popularity of *The Autobiography of Alice B. Toklas* helped make Gertrude Stein famous, her better-known protégé Ernest Hemingway wrote his own portrait of life in modernist Paris, focusing on a mere five years, from 1921 to 1926, and using the simple narrative voice he had adapted from Stein's own and made his stylistic trademark. A striking act of narrative imitation, *A Moveable Feast*, finished in 1960 and published posthumously, is a portrait of Paris itself, which Hemingway once characterized in those words. Unlike Stein's portrait, however, which seeks to undermine the coherence of identity and narrative even as it establishes an unforgettable narrative personality and narrative voice, Hemingway's portrait tries to shore up his identity and his voice, even as it becomes more and more apparent that a hole is opening up in the fabric of that coherence. Like Stein's *Autobiography*, Hemingway's *Feast* is deeply interested in establishing its author as a genius; like Stein's text, too, Hemingway's is focused on the wife that helped make his genius possible, in his case his first wife Hadley. Unlike Stein, however, Hemingway did not love his first wife enough to keep her, and the regret that permeates his memoir of their years together in Paris becomes so palpable that the text becomes less the portrait of the artist as a young man than it does a portrait of the artist as a failed husband— or at least, an artist whose literary success cannot compensate him in the end for the loss of his marriage.

As an act of imitation, Hemingway's *Feast* is striking on several fronts, not the least of which is his appropriation of the aesthetic texture of Stein's lesbian impersonation of Alice. He renders the Paris he remembers, as she does; he speaks simply, as she does; he attempts to convey character through observation, as she does; he is interested in establishing the fact of his genius, like her. Like Stein, too, he has a "wife" as counterpart to his "genius," and he also establishes his narrative reliability by rendering himself rendering the narrative, jumping back in time analeptically at the beginning of his text in a manner that seems to directly invoke *The Autobiography of Alice B. Toklas*. The question is not whether or not he is imitating Stein, because it is clear that he is imitating her. The question is, why? What does his imitation of Stein's imitation offer "to be seen"? If Stein's portrait deconstructs the masquerade of femininity as an imitation that reveals rather than conceals the lesbian, what does Hemingway's imitation of Stein's portrait produce?

The answer, in one notable place at least, is the disturbing substitution of violent masculine homophobia for Stein's lesbian impersonation. In a discussion of Stein's *The Making of Americans* where the narrator of *A Moveable Feast*—the bipolar consciousness "Hemingway" that the author assumes as his own—accuses her of authorial laziness and praises his own editorial efforts on her behalf: "For publication in the review I had to read all of Miss Stein's proof for her as this was a work which gave her no happiness."[15] At this point things get ugly:

> On this cold afternoon when I had come past the concierge's lodge and
> the cold courtyard to the warmth of the studio, all that was years ahead.

> On this day Miss Stein was instructing me about sex. By that time I had
> already learned that everything I did not understand probably had
> something to it. Miss Stein thought that I was too uneducated about sex
> and I must admit that I had certain prejudices against homosexuality
> since I knew its more primitive aspects. I knew it was why you carried
> a knife and would use it when you were in the company of tramps when
> you were a boy in the days when wolves was not a slang term for men
> obsessed by the pursuit of women. (18–19)

After a moment of prolepsis, or leaping forward in time, that could have
been lifted verbatim from *Alice B. Toklas*—"all that was years ahead"—
"Hemingway" sets out to destroy the myth of Stein's mentorship of him
as a young writer by reversing the terms of each of their relationships to
knowledge and wisdom. Instead of discussing Stein's literary opinions,
he has her lecture him on sex. This structure makes knowledge in this
context equivalent with sexual knowledge. Since Stein has no knowledge of what it is like to be a man, or a boy among men, her knowledge
is incomplete and inadequate, in Hemingway's terms. The inadequacy
of her knowledge is further accentuated by the text's association of her
with lesbianism: not only does she lack the knowledge of what it is to be
a man, but she lacks knowledge even of men. Under pretense of narration as explanation, Hemingway's speaker gets his digs in—at women,
at homosexuals, at Stein's class and gender propriety: "I could have
expressed myself more vividly by using an *inaccrochable* phrase that
wolves used on the lake boats, 'Oh gash may be fine but one eye for
mine.' But I was always careful of my language with Miss Stein even
when true phrases might have clarified or better expressed a prejudice"
(18–19).

Unlike Stein, "Hemingway" possesses the knowledge of what it is
to be a man, and—because he has also been a boy among "wolves"—he
also has a certain kind of feminine knowledge, the knowledge of what
it is to be hounded by men, and to have to defend one's self against
them. This gives him feminine knowledge, too, though his defensive but
threatening posture protects him from seeming feminized by it. And of
course, because he has a wife, he has sexual knowledge of women as
well. The ironic title of the chapter, "Miss Stein Instructs," further dis-
credits Stein as mentor. By rendering Stein's sexual sophistication as
naïve, gendered, and misguided, then, "Hemingway" explodes the
myth of Stein as his writing mentor, using her lesbianism as proof of her
inability to teach anybody anything useful about living in the world,
and, by implication, to teach anybody anything useful about writing.

The point of "Hemingway"'s attack on Stein's authority and sophistication is obvious: in a text that insists, as Stein's does, that one can
learn to write by studying Cézanne's paintings; that uses temporal
strategies of narrative validation strikingly similar to those found in
Alice B. Toklas; that similarly sets out to establish the author as genius
and the wife as muse; that draws literary portraits of the people and
places of modernist Paris in much the same way, the imitative act—
Hemingway's masquerade of Stein's masquerade—must be disavowed
as imitation and given the status of authenticity. His narrator does this
by means of the oldest trick in the book, the invocation of heterosexuality, and heterosexual masculinity, as the more authentic and universal
site of consciousness, along with the accompanying characterization of
homosexuality as limited, corrupt, immoral, and sterile. In the conversation that follows the description in *A Moveable Feast* of homosexual
predation among hoboes, his Stein attempts to justify lesbianism to him
as something vastly different from male homosexuality, arguing that
"the act male homosexuals commit is ugly and repugnant" while "In
women it is the opposite" (20). Though the narrator "Hemingway"
implies that there is no difference between the immorality of lesbians
and that of homosexual men, he cannot prove this himself, but relies
instead on trying to make Stein look as though she is contradicting the
logic of her own argument: "'I see,' I said. 'But what about so and so?'
'She's vicious,' Miss Stein said . . . 'She corrupts people'" (20).

Again, the terms of the reversal that he has set up strengthen the
difference not only between his sexuality and Stein's, his sophistication
and Stein's myopia, his status as a hard-working writer and Stein's laziness, and his clean marriage and Stein's sick relationship, but between
his *Moveable Feast* and Stein's *Autobiography of Alice B. Toklas*. In imitating a lesbian text of imitation while disavowing the imitation through
the assertion of homophobic violence, however, "Hemingway" reveals
his anxiety and renders his masculinity as a masquerade. He is not any
different from a woman in being the object of men's desire. Like the
women who refuse men, he structures his identity in terms of his refusal
of male advances; he has no sexual knowledge of them, and he justifies
his sexual views around the refusal of them: "Then all I had to be cured
of, I decided Miss Stein felt, was youth and loving my wife" (21). The
irony in his statement, of course, is that no one would see him as ever
having to be "cured" of anything so normal and healthy as loving his
wife, unless that person was mentally skewed. "I was not at all sad
when I got home to the rue Cardinal Lemoine and told my newly
acquired knowledge to my wife," the text relates sarcastically. "In the

night we were happy with our own knowledge we already had and other new knowledge we had acquired in the mountains" (21). Stein's sick knowledge, and the love letter to her wife that is *The Autobiography of Alice B. Toklas*, is reversed and rendered irrelevant, replaced by "Hemingway"'s normal healthy heterosexual uxoriousness.

Yet even given the text's irony, its insidious appeal to medical and social models of sexual normativity and homophobic violence, and its failed affectation of guilelessness, it is not so different from the modernist portraits of Stein, or of Colette. Imitating Stein's text while denying that such imitation is even possible, "Hemingway" both fakes it and fakes that he is faking it. How, then, is he different from the lesbians—Janet Flanner, Stein, Sylvia Beach—he seems proud to identify as his friends in *A Moveable Feast*? The answer is that he is not. Structuring his text so much like Stein's, he also finds himself pinning the narrative on a similar structure of genius and wife, artist and muse. The problem, however, is that his very insistence on sexual and moral difference, an insistence he uses to distance himself from Stein and her *Autobiography*, becomes the measure of his own failure to live up to these ideals. Unlike the texts of Colette and Stein that use love between women to explore the genius of wives, the wifeliness (masquerades) of genius, and ultimately, the imbrication of individual consciousnesses with their others, *A Moveable Feast* sets "Hemingway" up as the site of an authentic identity, one that anxiously fails him and the people who care about him. The whole of it takes shape around Paris as its center, but what Paris comes to stand for is, like Hemingway's "Hemingway," an illusion.

"Hemingway"'s Paris is supposed to be the place where hardworking, clean, normal young men become famous and live happily ever after with their fame and their families, while lazy lesbians decline into viciousness and obscurity and die, unremembered and alone. In the end, however, the very themes of innocence and knowledge "Hemingway" uses to validate his narrative authority and originality pull the rug out from under him, or, more accurately, pull "Paris" out of the center of the story, where it has functioned as a place-keeper for "Hemingway"'s own repressed sense of inauthenticity: "We always returned to it no matter who we were or how it was changed or with what difficulties, or ease, it could be reached. Paris was always worth it and you received return for whatever you brought to it. But this is how Paris was in the early days when we were very poor and very happy" (211).

The beauty of *A Moveable Feast*, the haunting resonance of its narrative self-portrait, lies in the way its impersonation becomes more and more aware of itself as a compensatory mask. But the tragedy of the novel is in its refusing itself the pleasures of its own impersonation, and its embrace of a "real" self that lies to itself about its own duplicity. Because of this its narrator, after vilifying almost all the people who had ever been kind to him, stands at the conclusion of the story in the empty place where the happy ending is supposed to be, or where "Hemingway" has indicated it should be, where the payoff of normative heterosexual masculinity should be his. Instead, all he has is lost: a city, friends, and young wife, all betrayed, all repudiated, all of whom once made possible the man he might have become, and did not.

The self-conscious impersonation that fakes it in modernism, then, is a far cry from the "extinction of personality" Eliot advocates in "Tradition and the Individual Talent," where the artist emulates a certain kind of "fitting in" and strives to reconcile individual expression with the artistic and cultural conventions of "the mind of Europe."[16] Instead, "faking it" is a self-conscious, perverse deployment of personality as style against the censuring look that seeks to contain and normalize all personalities. "Faking it" celebrates grand selves and multiple selves rather than diminished ones. In faking it, invention and pleasure go hand in hand, and the drama of castration-as-convention is turned on its ear, sent up, acted out as a role and an artifice that anyone can approximate—or refuse. Colette ends *The Pure and the Impure* much as she began it, with the "trembling" and "plaintive" sound of a woman's voice. Only this time the woman is saying the word "pure," which the narrator admits "has never revealed an intelligible meaning for me" (175). The narrator concludes: "I can only use the word to quench an optical thirst for purity in the transparencies that evoke it—in bubbles, in a volume of water, and in the imaginary latitudes entrenched, beyond reach, at the center of a dense crystal" (176). Purity—like the femininity it is supposed to describe, and be described by in turn—is only interesting inasmuch as it suggests the things beyond it, things of the imagination and of poetry, and of the desire for beauty that gives pleasure outside of social abstractions. The "optical thirst" of the artist becomes the definition of the word, and the seenness of the sitter—a seenness that dissolves into style as the beauty of things named by the narrator in approximation of elusive meaning—is revealed as the "real" subject and real meaning of artistic representation.

Janet Flanner wearing Nancy Cunard's father's top hat, photographed by Berenice Abbott (1927). Library of Congress. © Berenice Abbott/Commerce Graphics Ltd., NYC.

AFTERWORD

LOOKING BACK:
MODERNISM WAS YESTERDAY

Janet Flanner's "belated" praise of Josephine Baker's opening night performance in her re-edited collection of her jazz-era *New Yorker* columns, the 1972 volume *Paris Was Yesterday,* performs a supremely modernist gesture in its revisioning of the past in the very act of looking back on it. When as Paris correspondent "Genet" she first reviewed the 1925 *La Revue Negre* performance that made Josephine Baker famous, she breezily dismissed the ethnic history of the production's cast with the same nonchalance she employed to describe its sets: "Covarrubias did the sets, pink drops with cornucopias of hams and watermelons, and the Civil War did the rest, aided by Miss Baker. The music is tuneless and stunningly orchestrated, and the end of the show is dull, but never Miss Baker's part."[1] "Genet"'s unfunny act of laughing off slavery and its aftermath was no doubt part of the reason for Flanner's retraction and addendum, written much later in the introduction to *Paris Was Yesterday,* which collected the sketches of Paris life she wrote between 1925 and 1939. The "new type of journalistic foreign correspondence" (xix) Flanner helped invent in her fortnightly "Letter from Paris" for the *New Yorker* looks a lot like modernist literary portraiture. The letters consist mainly of sketches of artistic, literary, and theatrical personalities, as well as an occasional crime story. "Genet"'s style of telling emphasizes the self-conscious eye of the beholder as well as the character of the beheld: "Criticism, to be valid, in my opinion," she writes, "demanded a certain personal aspect or slant of the writer's mind" (xx).

However, in the apology for the Baker review she wrote nearly fifty years later, Flanner paradoxically insists on inventing her old self anew, its consciousness cured of its racial insensitivity by the post–Civil Rights

115

era. "I wrote about it timidly, uncertainly, and like a dullard" (xx), she apologizes, nevertheless insisting that "Josephine Baker . . . remains to me now like a still-fresh vision, sensual, exciting and isolated in my memory today, almost fifty years later." Having established the fiction of a "fresh vision," she introduces her memory of Baker as both tribute and eyewitness reportage: "So here follows what I should have written then about her appearance, as a belated tribute" (xx).

This is a remarkable statement on its own, claiming as it does a rela- tionship to the past that is both mediated by the judgment of history and free of it. "Genet"'s/Flanner's fashioned past and fashioned self are always aware of being read, of being seen. However, like "Hem- ingway"'s insistent hunt for an authentic self, Flanner's claim to possess an immediacy of vision nearly fifty years after the fact creates an oscil- lating self-consciousness that both supports and fails to support the por- traitist's claim that she is drawing from life. In this oscillation one begins to see a shift away from a more stylized and particular self-seeing and toward a more public eye, one attuned to both celebrity and the political values of U.S. culture and counterculture in the wake of the Vietnam War and the Civil Rights movement. Ostensibly in tribute to Baker's personality and celebrity, but also, one senses, to redress a guilty con- science that her failure to appreciate Baker at the time was due to racist condescension, Flanner does Flanner "doing" Genet once more, describing Baker on stage as if seeing her for the first time:

> She made her entry entirely nude except for a pink flamingo feather between her limbs; she was being carried upside down and doing the split on the shoulder of a black giant. Midstage he paused, and with his long fingers holding her basket-wise around the waist, swung her in a slow cartwheel to the stage floor, where she stood, like his magnificent discarded burden, in an instant of complete silence. She was an unfor- gettable female ebony statue. A scream of salutation spread through the theater. (xx)

"Genet"'s layered, doubled persona that "witnesses" Josephine Baker's act a half-century later creates a Dorian Gray or Alice B. Toklas kind of self, a self out of time and autonomous as "Genet," yet at the same time a part of history as Janet Flanner. It is readily apparent that this self is limited even if its intentions are good, and this limitation shuts down the pleasure of the voice occupying its own theatrical per- formance. The idiosyncratic, stylized particular eye must give way to a public look with—it can be hoped—more evolved social values. Flanner doing "Genet" still manages to characterize both of the dancers as freakish—though striking—objects, dehumanizing them with her look even as she celebrates them. But Flanner doing "Flanner" intervenes, stopping the eyewitness narrative by insisting "Whatever happened next was unimportant" because "the acute response of the white masculine public" to Baker's body was proof that for the French, "black was beautiful" (xx). With the interjection of this 1960s slogan, "Genet"'s political redress crumbles once more with the report of "Negro choruses" drunk on fame and champagne on stage, though "nevertheless alive and creative with the integral talent of their race and training" (xxi). The portraitist's voice here that is the mix of both "Genet" and "Flanner" slyly adds that as Baker's career "ripened" she appeared in her "famous festoon of bananas," concluding that "She was the established new American star for Europe" (xxi).

While it can be argued that Flanner/"Genet" makes things worse rather than better by revisiting the scene of Baker's Paris triumph and reiterating her own well-meaning yet inept racial politics, her act of revision is significant not only in its acknowledgment of former bias on her part, but in the way her own character diminishes itself in its self-conscious faltering. In "doing" Genet once more, she recaptures some of the pleasure of speaking as that person, of hearing herself talking, that characterized the voice of the Paris letters. At the same time, the refashioning of that voice displaces its pleasurable occupation of itself from the personality of the speaker back to the public, and in doing so acknowledges rather than deflects the gaze, in an attempt at an ethics, however clumsy, that her earlier personality failed to embody. Self-scrutiny has necessarily intervened in the pleasure that voice once took in its own playfulness, and it is striking to see the constructedness and the limits of that pleasure exposed here, in a moment of self-consciousness quite different—though not meaningfully different enough—from the one that initially fashioned "Genet."

But pleasure and ethics do not have to oppose each other, and it is one of the arguments of this book that it is in modernism's textual and iconic interaction with the dynamics of visual culture that the pleasure modernism takes in itself can be ethical as well. One of the most striking visual portraits we have of Janet Flanner remains the Berenice Abbott photograph of Flanner in white trousers with pinstripes, a pale shirt with French cuffs and cufflinks, a dark overcoat, and Nancy Cunard's father's dove-gray top hat, upon which two masks sit, one white, one black. Flanner's dandified dress, short, graying hair, and theatrical masks all accentuate the dramatic contrasts of black and white that characterize this print. She looks mannish but stylish, smart, queer, theatrical, and self-conscious. Her eyes are dark and a little sad, her face is starkly white, and her mouth turns up almost sardonically at one corner, like the fool or harlequin of an older time. She is posing, and the masks on her hat suggest several invented and strategic personalities. The fact that this top hat belonged to an international shipping magnate contrasts deliciously with these masks, white on top of black in a kind of racial pecking order, whose elastic straps now circle the hat as the Cunard line circled the globe. These masks not only usurp the hat and redefine it for the purposes of the portrait, but as racial masks they work alongside Flanner's masculine cross-dressing to undermine the notion of authentic identity in favor of theatrical self-presentation. Cunard's daughter Nancy scandalized high society with her political work opposing racial injustice and her publication of the sweeping anthology *Negro*. Flanner's wearing of the hat with its black and white masks stages her alliance with Nancy Cunard in the project of usurping the white wealthy patriarch's authority, in this case through lesbian appropriation and reinvention of the patriarch's masculine style.

Today we see this photograph as a photograph of Janet Flanner having fun with her friend Berenice; Janet Flanner, celebrity correspondent, literary personality and critic, and friend of Hemingway; Janet Flanner, left-leaning, Left Bank lesbian and lover of Solita Solano. What we forget, or dismiss as playfulness or portrait convention, is that this is a portrait of Janet Flanner doing and undoing a portrait of Janet Flanner, a making and unmaking of the notion of personality that confronts the viewer with the dynamism of the portrait itself. This is not to say that readers and viewers today do not recognize the performative gestures of modernist portraiture, but that in our historical remove from it, we need to remember that the meta-discursive nature of modernism insists upon pleasure and perversity as it watches itself watching its own artistic inventiveness and innovation. The self-reflexivity of this may lead to the ethical reconsideration of modernist aesthetic pleasure, as it does for Flanner, and—though his ethics takes a conservative rather than progressive turn—Hemingway. But the ethics of self-conscious perversity lie mainly in its refusal of normativity and celebration of stylized self-elaboration and impersonation, rather than in any straightforward social agenda. What intrigues and troubles so many readers of these texts resembles the ambivalence with which many of us view lesbian, gay, bisexual, transgendered, and queer culture(s) today, an ambivalence due in large part to the simultaneous invitation and evasion of politics, the interplay of identity, desire, and pleasure, that characterizes both the style of queer "modernist" portraiture and the making, unmaking, and remaking of subjects in erotic communities. The ethical failures of modernist-era artists—Radclyffe Hall's patronizing racial, class, and sexual chauvinisms; T. S. Eliot's fascist sympathies; Natalie Barney's anti-Semitism; Gertrude Stein's Vichy collaboration—exist alongside the dynamism of its portraiture, a dynamism where the object of looking insists on looking back, one that circulates beauty, sexual desire, and a longing for justice, and often questions the very basis—normative individual identity—upon which so many oppressions are launched. This troubled, doubled look, this insistence on the pleasures of self-consciousness, this bold appropriation of the look of posterity as well as contemporary scrutiny, is what remains compelling about these portraits, and this is why the smile, the pose, the sardonic look with which they confront spectators continues to intrigue us with its suggestion of knowledge, bravado, and pleasure, as these portraits continue to seduce readers, over and over again, back into their queer world.

NOTES

INTRODUCTION

1. Shari Benstock, *Women of the Left Bank: Paris, 1900–1940* (Austin: University of Texas Press, 1986), 31.

2. Ibid., 32.

3. Sandra Gilbert and Susan Gubar, *No Man's Land: The Place of the Woman Writer in the Twentieth Century, Volume 1: The War of the Words* (New Haven, Conn.: Yale University Press, 1988), xii.

4. Lisa Rado, "Lost and Found: Remembering Modernism, Rethinking Feminism," in Lisa Rado, ed., *Rereading Modernism: New Directions in Feminist Criticism* (New York: Garland, 1994), 4.

5. Eve Kosofsky Sedgwick, *Epistemology of the Closet* (Berkeley: University of California Press, 1990), 1.

6. Melissa Bradshaw, "Remembering Amy Lowell," in Melissa Bradshaw and Adrienne Munich, eds., *Amy Lowell, American Modern* (New Brunswick, N.J.: Rutgers University Press, 2004), 167–85.

7. Hugh Kenner, *The Pound Era* (Berkeley: University of California Press, 1971), 382.

8. See Adrienne Munich and Melissa Bradshaw's Introduction to their *Amy Lowell, American Modern*, xiv.

9. Hugh Kenner, *A Sinking Island: The Modern English Writers* (Baltimore, Md.: Johns Hopkins University Press, 1987), 13.

10. Ibid., 14.

11. Maude Ellmann, *The Poetics of Impersonality: T. S. Eliot and Ezra Pound* (Cambridge, Mass.: Harvard University Press, 1987), 4.

12. Virginia Woolf, "Mr. Bennett and Mrs. Brown," in Leonard Woolf, ed., *Collected Essays* (Toronto: Hogarth Press Ltd., 1966), 1:319–37.

13. Virginia Woolf, "Personalities," in Leonard Woolf, ed., *Collected Essays*, 2:273–77.

14. See Michael Levenson's discussion of Irving Babbit, in *A Genealogy of Modernism: A Study of English Literary Doctrine, 1908–1922* (Cambridge: Cambridge University Press, 1984), 28–30.

15. See Sedgwick, *Epistemology of the Closet*, 2; also see Jonathan Ned Katz, *The Invention of Heterosexuality* (New York: Plume, 1995).

16. Joseph Bristow, *Effeminate England: Homoerotic Writing after 1885* (New York: Columbia University Press, 1995), 2.

17. Marcel Proust, *Swann's Way: Remembrance of Things Past*, translated by C. K. Scott Moncrieff and Terence Kilmartin (New York: Vintage, 1989), 175–76. Parenthetical references to this work refer to this edition.

18. D. H. Lawrence, *Women in Love* (New York: Penguin, 1983 [1920]), 71. Parenthetical references to this work refer to this edition.

19. Gertrude Stein, *The Autobiography of Alice B. Toklas*, in Catharine R. Stimpson and Harriet Chessman, eds., *Stein: Writings, 1903–1932* (New York: Library of America, 1998), 669. Parenthetical references to this work refer to this edition.

CHAPTER 1

1. I use this term advisedly, knowing full well that sexual inversion, rather than homosexuality, was the dominant paradigm for understanding same-sex sexual attraction and non-normative gender behavior in this era. However, the term and concept of "homosexuality" was invented at this time (around 1892, according to Jonathan Ned Katz, *Invention of Heterosexuality*) as part of the invention of an equally pathologized "heterosexuality." That notion of "homosexuality" as same-sex sexual attraction retains much of its original meaning today, though "heterosexuality" no longer implies the bisexuality it once did. As such, it does not seem to me to be historically inaccurate to suggest that Wilde's notion of a community of men erotically and intellectually attracted to other men (yet not necessarily possessing feminine gender traits themselves) resembles latter-day notions of homosexuality far more than it does the concept of sexual and gender inversion popular in his era.

2. Oscar Wilde, *The Picture of Dorian Gray*, in Merlin Holland, ed., *Collins Complete Works of Oscar Wilde Centenary Edition* (New York: HarperCollins, 1999), 18. Parenthetical references to this work refer to this edition.

3. Sedgwick, *Epistemology of the Closet*, 165.

4. See Jonathan Dollimore, *Sexual Dissence: Augustine to Wilde, Freud to Foucault* (Oxford: Clarendon Press, 1991).

5. Gregory W. Bredbeck, "Narcissus in the Wilde: Textual Cathexis and the Origins of Queer Camp," in Moe Meyer, ed., *The Politics and Poetics of Camp* (New York: Routledge, 1994), 57.

6. Neil Bartlett, *Who Was That Man? A Present for Mr. Oscar Wilde* (London: Serpent's Tail, 1988), 31–32.

7. Sedgwick, *Epistemology of the Closet*, 160.

8. Moe Meyer, "Under the Sign of Wilde: An Archaeology of Posing," in Meyer, *Politics and Poetics of Camp*, 87–88.

9. Richard Ellmann, *Oscar Wilde* (New York: Vintage, 1988 [1984]), 278.

10. Jeffrey Weeks, *Sex, Politics, and Society: The Regulation of Sexuality since 1800* (London: Longman, 1989), 106.

11. Ellmann, *Oscar Wilde*, 435.

12. Dick Hebdige, *Hiding in the Light* (New York: Routledge, 1989). It is important to note that Hebdige's theory of subcultural resistance through style is anchored in large part to homosexual style, specifically to the queer use to which the writer Genet put a tube of Vaseline. See Dick Hebdige, *Subculture: The Meaning of Style* (New York: Routledge, 1981).

13. Whistler's name appeared in the original draft as the murdered painter Basil Hallward (Ellmann, *Oscar Wilde*, 278).
14. Ellen Moers, *The Dandy: Brummell to Beerbohm* (New York: Viking, 1960), 288.
15. Ellmann, *Oscar Wilde*, 79.
16. Meyer, "Under the Sign," 77.
17. Moers, *The Dandy*, 17.
18. Ibid.
19. Jacques Lacan, *The Four Fundamental Concepts of Psycho-Analysis*, ed. Jacques-Alain Miller, translated by Alan Sheridan (London/New York: W. W. Norton, 1981), 62. Parenthetical references to this work refer to this edition.
20. Shari Benstock points out Lacan's debt to modernist literature in "Paris Lesbianism and the Politics of Reaction, 1900–1940," in Martin Duberman, Martha Vicinus, and George Chauncey Jr., eds., *Hidden from History: Reclaiming the Gay and Lesbian Past* (New York: Meridian, 1990 [1989]), 335.
21. Ellie Ragland, "Lacan and the *Hommosexuelle*: 'A Love Letter,'" in Tim Dean and Christopher Lane, eds., *Homosexuality and Psychoanalysis* (Chicago: University of Chicago Press, 2001), 106.
22. Sigmund Freud, "On Narcissism: An Introduction (1914)," in Philip Rieff, ed., *The Collected Papers of Sigmund Freud: General Psychological Theory* (New York: Macmillan [Collier], 1963), 56. All quotations in this paragraph come from page 56.
23. Steven Bruhm, *Reflecting Narcissus: A Queer Aesthetic* (Minneapolis: University of Minnesota Press, 2001), 15.
24. For an excellent scholarly history of queer work on narcissism and Narcissus, as well as the elaboration of Narcissus as "the figure who rejects" (15), see Bruhm, *Reflecting Narcissus*
25. Henri F. Ellenberger, *The Discovery of the Unconscious: The History and Evolution of Dynamic Psychiatry* (New York: Basic Books, 1970).
26. Sigmund Freud, *Three Essays on the Theory of Sexuality*, translated and edited by James Strachey (New York: Basic Books, 1962), 42.
27. Sigmund Freud, *Leonard da Vinci and a Memory of His Childhood*, translated by Alan Tyson, edited by James Strachey (New York: Norton, 1962), 19. Subsequent parenthetical references to this work are to this edition.
28. Oscar Wilde, "The Portrait of Mr. W. H.," in Merlin Holland, ed., *Collins Complete Works of Oscar Wilde Centenary Edition* (New York: HarperCollins, 1999), 302–3. Parenthetical references to this story refer to this edition.

CHAPTER 2

1. Donald Crafton, *The Talkies: American Cinema's Transition to Sound, 1926–1931* (Berkeley: University of California Press, 1997).
2. Scott Eyman, *The Speed of Sound: Hollywood and the Talkie Revolution, 1926–1930* (Baltimore, Md.: Johns Hopkins University Press, 1997), 136.
3. Susan Sontag, "Notes on Camp," in *A Susan Sontag Reader* (New York: Vintage, 1983), 109.
4   Ellie Ragland, "The Relation between the Voice and the Gaze," in

Richard Feldstein, Bruce Fink, and Maire Jaanus, eds., *Reading Seminar XI: Lacan's Four Fundamental Concepts of Psychoanalysis* (Albany: SUNY Press, 1995), 197.

5. Kaja Silverman, *The Acoustic Mirror: The Female Voice in Psychoanalysis and Cinema* (Bloomington: Indiana University Press, 1988), 43.

6. Slavoj Zizek, "'I Hear You with My Eyes'; or, The Invisible Master," in Renata Salecl and Slavoj Zizek, eds., *Gaze and Voice as Love Objects* (Durham, N.C.: Duke University Press, 1996), 92.

7. Michel Foucault, *The History of Sexuality: An Introduction Volume One* New York: Random House [Vintage], 1990), 12.

8. Michael North, *The Dialectic of Modernism: Race, Language and Twentieth-Century Literature* (New York: Oxford University Press, 1994), 11.

9. Ibid.

10. See Henri F. Ellenberger, *The Discovery of the Unconscious: The History and Evolution of Dynamic Psychiatry* (New York: Basic Books, 1970), 480–89.

11. Robert Graves and Alan Hodge, *The Long Week-End: A Social History of Great Britain, 1918–1939* (New York: Norton, 1963 [1940]), 102.

12. Hugh Kenner, *The Invisible Poet: T. S. Eliot* (New York: Harcourt, Brace & World, 1959), 4.

13. Radclyffe Hall, *The Well of Loneliness* (London: Virago, 1982 [1928]), 247. Parenthetical references to this work refer to this edition.

14. Djuna Barnes, *Nightwood* (New York: New Directions, 1961 [1937]), 162–63. Parenthetical references to this work refer to this edition.

15. Langston Hughes, *Selected Poems of Langston Hughes* (New York: Vintage, 1990), 201. All references are to this edition.

16. Arnold Rampersad, "Madam Alberta K. Johnson," in William L. Andrews, Frances Smith Foster, and Trudier Harris, eds., *The Oxford Companion to African American Literature* (New York: Oxford University Press, 1997), 468.

17. Ibid.

CHAPTER 3

1. Wyndham Lewis, *Men Without Art* (London: Black Sparrow Press, 1987 [1934]), 118.

2. Hugh Kenner, "Wyndham Lewis: The Satirist as Barbarian," in Claude Rowson, ed., *English Satire and the Satiric Tradition* (Oxford: Blackwell, 1984), 264.

3. Wyndham Lewis, *The Apes of God* (London: The Arthur Press, 1930; New York: Penguin, 1965), 233. Parenthetical citations of this novel refer to this edition.

4. Compton Mackenzie, *Extraordinary Women* (New York: Macy-Masius/The Vanguard Press, 1928), 41. Parenthetical citations of this novel refer to this edition.

5. My thanks to The Modern Language Association for permission to reprint this section which appeared in a longer form as "Kissing a Negress in the Dark": Englishness as a Masquerade in Virginia Woolf's *Orlando*," *PMLA* 112:3 (May 1997): 393–404.

6. Vera Brittain, *Radclyffe Hall: A Case of Obscenity?* (South Brunswick: Barnes, 1969), 100.

7. Virginia Woolf, *The Diary of Virginia Woolf,* vol. 3, ed. Anne Olivier Bell (New York: Harcourt, 1980), 131.

8. Pamela Caughie, *Virginia Woolf and Postmodernism: Literature in Quest and Question of Itself* (Urbana: University of Illinois Press, 1991), XX: 81.

9. Virginia Woolf, *Orlando* (New York: Harcourt, 1980 [1928]), XX: 1. Parenthetical citations of this work refer to this edition.

10. Djuna Barnes, *Ladies Almanack: showing their Signs and their tides; their Moons and their Changes; the Seasons as it is with them; their Eclipses and Equinoxes; as well as a full Record of diurnal and nocturnal Distempers* (Normal, Ill.: Dalkey Archive Press, 1992 [1928]), 6. Parenthetical citations of this novel refer to this edition.

CHAPTER 4

1. Catharine R. Stimpson, "Gertrude Stein and the Lesbian Lie," in Margo Culley, ed., *American Women's Autobiography: Fea(s)ts of Memory* (Madison: University of Wisconsin Press, 1992), 153.

2. Colette, *The Pure and the Impure,* translated by Herma Briffault (New York: Farrar, Straus and Giroux, 1984), 8–9. Parenthetical citations of this work refer to this edition.

3. Marie Carmichael Stopes, *Married Love* (New York: Eugenics Publishing Co., 1931 [1918]), 32.

4. See Christina Simmons, "Companionate Marriage and the Lesbian Threat," *Frontiers* 4:3 (Fall 1979): 55. See also Lillian Faderman, *Odd Girls and Twilight Lovers: A History of Lesbian Life in Twentieth-Century America* (New York: Columbia University Press, 1991), 90–91, and John D'Emilio and Estelle B. Freedman, *Intimate Matters: A History of Sexuality in America* (New York: Harper & Row, 1988), 257.

5. The most well-known recent use of Riviere appears in Judith Butler's long discussion of "Womanliness as a Masquerade" in her book *Gender Trouble* (New York: Routledge, 1991), a book seen by many as inaugurating academic "queer theory." Riviere is crucial to Butler's notion of gender as performance, but even as she extends Riviere's radical insight that there is no femininity outside the masquerade of femininity, Butler searches for depths, and at one point she even queries, "But does Riviere know the homosexuality of the woman in masquerade that she describes?" (52). This search for interiorities and essences, for the "sexual orientation or desire" (52), "melancholic identification" (50), and "sexual fantasy" (54) indicative of deep identity, is at odds with the way of being modern that Riviere observes and describes.

6. Stephen Heath, "Joan Riviere and the Masquerade," in Victor Burgin, James Donald, and Cora Kaplan, eds., *Formations of Fantasy* (London: Routledge, 1986), 45.

7. Joan Riviere, "Womanliness as a Masquerade," in Burgin et al., *Formations of Fantasy,* 38.

8. Robert Samuels, "Art and the Position of the Analyst," in Feldstein et al., *Reading Seminar XI,* 184.

9. Ellie Ragland, "The Relation between the Voice and the Gaze," in Feldstein et al., *Reading Seminar XI*, 190.

10. Edouard Bourdet, *The Captive* (New York: Brentano's, 1926), XX: 149–50. Parenthetical citations of this work refer to this edition.

11. Nella Larsen, *Passing,* in Deborah McDowell, ed., Quicksand *and* Passing (New Brunswick, N.J.: Rutgers University Press, 1989 [1986]), XX: 221. Parenthetical citations of this work refer to this edition.

12. Stimpson, "Gertrude Stein and the Lesbian Lie," 157–58.

13. Georgia Johnston, "Narratologies of Pleasure: Gertrude Stein's *The Autobiography of Alice B. Toklas,*" *Modern Fiction Studies* 42:3 (1996): 560–606.

14. One of the best discussions of their relationship remains Catharine Stimpson's "Gertice/Altrude: Stein, Toklas, and the Paradox of the Happy Marriage," in Ruth Perry and Martine Watson Brownley, eds., *Mothering the Mind: Twelve Studies of Writers and Their Silent Partners* (New York: Holmes and Meier, 1984).

15. Ernest Hemingway, *A Moveable Feast* (New York: Simon and Schuster, 1996 [1964]), 18. Parenthetical citations of this work refer to this edition.

16. T. S. Eliot, "Tradition and the Individual Talent," in Frank Kermode, ed., *Selected Prose of T. S. Eliot* (New York: Harcourt Brace Jovanovich/Farrar, Straus and Giroux, 1975), 39. Parenthetical citations of this essay refer to this edition.

AFTERWORD

1. Janet Flanner, *Paris Was Yesterday, 1925–1939* (New York: Harvest/Harcourt Brace Jovanovich, 1988 [1972]), 3. Parenthetical citations of this work refer to this edition.

BIBLIOGRAPHY

Barnes, Djuna. *Ladies Almanack: showing their Signs and their tides; their Moons and their Changes; the Seasons as it is with them; their Eclipses and Equinoxes; as well as a full Record of diurnal and nocturnal Distempers.* Normal, Ill.: Dalkey Archive Press, 1992 [1928].

———. *Nightwood.* New York: New Directions, 1961 [1937].

Bartlett, Neil. *Who Was That Man? A Present for Mr. Oscar Wilde.* London: Serpent's Tail, 1988.

Benstock, Shari. "Paris Lesbianism and the Politics of Reaction, 1900–1940." In Martin Duberman, Martha Vicinus, and George Chauncey Jr., eds., *Hidden from History: Reclaiming the Gay and Lesbian Past,* 332–46. New York: Meridian, 1990 [1989].

———. *Women of the Left Bank: Paris, 1900–1940.* Austin: University of Texas Press, 1986.

Boone, Joseph. *Libidinal Currents: Sexuality and the Shaping of Modernism.* Chicago: University of Chicago Press, 1998.

Bourdet, Edouard. *The Captive.* New York: Brentano's, 1926.

Bradshaw, Melissa. "Remembering Amy Lowell." In Melissa Bradshaw and Adrienne Munich, eds., *Amy Lowell, American Modern,* 167–85. New Brunswick, N.J.: Rutgers University Press, 2004.

Bredbeck, Gregory W. "Narcissus in the Wilde: Textual Cathexis and the Origins of Queer Camp." In Moe Meyer, ed., *The Politics and Poetics of Camp,* 51–74. New York: Routledge, 1994.

Bristow, Joseph. *Effeminate England: Homoerotic Writing After 1885.* New York: Columbia University Press, 1995.

Brittain, Vera. *Radclyffe Hall: A Case of Obscenity?* South Brunswick, UK: Barnes, 1969.

Bruhm, Steven. *Reflecting Narcissus: A Queer Aesthetic.* Minneapolis: University of Minnesota Press, 2001.

Butler, Judith. *Bodies That Matter: On the Discursive Limits of "Sex."* New York: Routledge, 1993.

———. *Gender Trouble: Feminism and the Subversion of Identity.* New York: Routledge, 1991.

Caughie, Pamela. *Virginia Woolf and Postmodernism: Literature in Quest and Question of Itself.* Urbana: University of Illinois Press, 1991.

Colette. *The Pure and the Impure.* Translated by Herma Briffault. New York: Farrar, Straus and Giroux, 1984.

Crafton, Donald. *The Talkies: American Cinema's Transition to Sound, 1926–1931.* Berkeley: University of California Press, 1997.

DeKoven, Marianne. *Rich and Strange: Gender, History, Modernism.* Princeton, N.J.: Princeton University Press, 1991.

D'Emilio, John, and Estelle B. Freedman. *Intimate Matters: A History of Sexuality in America.* New York: Harper & Row, 1988.

Dollimore, Jonathan. *Sexual Dissidence: Augustine to Wilde, Freud to Foucault.* Oxford: Clarendon Press, 1991.

Eliot, T. S. "Tradition and the Individual Talent." In Frank Kermode, ed., *Selected Prose of T. S. Eliot,* 37–44. New York: Harcourt Brace Jovanovich/Farrar, Straus and Giroux, 1975.

Ellenberger, Henri F. *The Discovery of the Unconscious: The History and Evolution of Dynamic Psychiatry.* New York: Basic Books, 1970.

Ellmann, Maude. *The Poetics of Impersonality: T. S. Eliot and Ezra Pound.* Cambridge, Mass.: Harvard University Press, 1987.

Ellmann, Richard. *Oscar Wilde.* New York: Vintage, 1988 [1984].

Eyman, Scott. *The Speed of Sound: Hollywood and the Talkie Revolution, 1926–1930.* Baltimore, Md.: Johns Hopkins University Press, 1997.

Faderman, Lillian. *Odd Girls and Twilight Lovers: A History of Lesbian Life in Twentieth-Century America.* New York: Columbia University Press, 1991.

Flanner, Janet. *Paris Was Yesterday, 1925–1939.* New York: Harvest/Harcourt Brace Jovanovich, 1988 [1972].

Foucault, Michel. *The History of Sexuality: An Introduction Volume One.* New York: Vintage, 1990.

Freud, Sigmund. *Leonardo da Vinci and a Memory of His Childhood.* Translated by Alan Tyson. New York: W. W. Norton, 1964.

———. "On Narcissism: An Introduction (1914)." In Philip Rieff, ed., *The Collected Papers of Sigmund Freud: General Psychological Theory,* 56–82. New York: Macmillan [Collier], 1963.

Gilbert, Sandra, and Susan Gubar. *No Man's Land: The Place of the Woman Writer in the Twentieth Century. Volume 1: The War of the Words.* New Haven, Conn.: Yale University Press, 1988.

Graves, Robert, and Alan Hodge. *The Long Week-End: A Social History of Great Britain, 1918–1937.* New York: Norton, 1963 [1940].

Halberstam, Judith. *Female Masculinity.* Durham, N.C.: Duke University Press, 1998.

Hall, Radclyffe. *The Well of Loneliness.* London: Virago, 1982 [1928].

Halpern, Richard. *Shakespeare's Perfume: Sodomy and Sublimity in the Sonnets, Wilde, Freud, and Lacan.* Philadelphia: University of Pennsylvania Press, 2002.

Heath, Stephen. "Joan Riviere and the Masquerade." In Victor Burgin, James Donald, and Cora Kaplan, eds., *Formations of Fantasy,* 45–61. London: Routledge, 1986.

Hebdige, Dick. *Hiding in the Light.* New York: Routledge, 1989.

———. *Subculture: The Meaning of Style.* New York: Routledge, 1981.

Hemingway, Ernest. *A Moveable Feast.* New York: Simon and Schuster, 1996 [1964].

Herrmann, Anne. *Queering the Moderns: Poses/Portraits/Performances.* New York: Palgrave, 2000.

Hovey, Jaime. "Kissing a Negress in the Dark": Englishness as a Masquerade in Virginia Woolf's *Orlando*." *PMLA* 112:3 (May 1997): 393–404.

Hughes, Langston. *Selected Poems of Langston Hughes*. New York: Vintage, 1990.

Jacobs, Karen. *The Mind's Eye: Literary Modernism and Visual Culture*. Ithaca, N.Y.: Cornell University Press, 2001.

Johnston, Georgia. "Narratologies of Pleasure: Gertrude Stein's *The Autobiography of Alice B. Toklas*." *Modern Fiction Studies* 42:3 (1996): 560–606.

Katz, Jonathan Ned. *The Invention of Heterosexuality*. New York: Plume, 1995.

Kenner, Hugh. *The Invisible Poet: T. S. Eliot*. New York: Harcourt, Brace & World, 1959.

———. *The Pound Era*. Berkeley: University of California Press, 1971.

———. *A Sinking Island: The Modern English Writers*. Baltimore, Md.: Johns Hopkins University Press, 1987.

———. "Wyndham Lewis: The Satirist as Barbarian." In Claude Rowson, ed., *English Satire and the Satiric Tradition*, 264–75. Oxford: Blackwell, 1984.

Lacan, Jacques. *The Four Fundamental Concepts of Psycho-Analysis*. Edited by Jacques-Alain Miller, translated by Alan Sheridan. London: W. W. Norton, 1981.

Lamos, Colleen. *Deviant Modernism: Sexual and Textual Errancy in T. S. Eliot, James Joyce, and Marcel Proust*. Cambridge: Cambridge University Press, 1998.

Larsen, Nella. *Passing*. In Deborah McDowell, ed., *Quicksand and Passing*. New Brunswick, N.J.: Rutgers University Press, 1989 [1986].

Lawrence, D. H. *Women in Love*. New York: Penguin, 1983 [1920].

Levensen, Michael. *A Genealogy of Modernism: A Study of English Literary Doctrine, 1908–1922*. Cambridge: Cambridge University Press, 1984.

Lewis, Wyndham. *The Apes of God*. London: Arthur Press, 1930; New York: Penguin, 1965.

———. *Men Without Art*. London: Black Sparrow Press, 1987 [1934].

Mackenzie, Compton. *Extraordinary Women*. New York: Macy-Masius/The Vanguard Press, 1928.

McDowell, Deborah. "Introduction." In Nella Larsen, *Quicksand and Passing*. Edited by Deborah McDowell. New Brunswick, N.J.: Rutgers University Press, 1986.

Meyer, Moe. "Under the Sign of Wilde: An Archaeology of Posing." In Moe Meyer, ed., *The Politics and Poetics of Camp*, 75–109. New York: Routledge, 1994.

Moers, Ellen. *The Dandy: Brummell to Beerbohm*. New York: Viking, 1960.

Nicholls, Peter. *Modernisms: A Literary Guide*. Berkeley: University of California Press, 1995.

North, Michael. *The Dialectic of Modernism: Race, Language, and Twentieth-Century Literature*. New York: Oxford University Press, 1994.

Proust, Marcel. *Swann's Way: Remembrance of Things Past*. Translated by C. K. Scott Moncrieff and Terence Kilmartin. New York: Vintage, 1989.

Rado, Lisa. "Lost and Found: Remembering Modernism, Rethinking Feminism." In Lisa Rado, ed., *Rereading Modernism: New Directions in Feminist Criticism*, 3–19. New York: Garland, 1994.

Ragland, Ellie. "Lacan and the *Hommosexuelle*: 'A Love Letter.'" In Tim Dean and Christopher Lane, eds., *Homosexuality and Psychoanalysis,* 98–119. Chicago: University of Chicago Press, 2001.

——. "The Relation between the Voice and the Gaze." In Richard Feldstein, Bruce Fink, and Maire Jaanus, eds., *Reading Seminar XI: Lacan's Four Fundamental Concepts of Psychoanalysis,* 187–203. Albany: SUNY Press, 1995.

Rampersad, Arnold. "Madam Alberta K. Johnson." In William L. Andrews, Frances Smith Foster, and Trudier Harris, eds., *The Oxford Companion to African American Literature,* 468. New York: Oxford University Press, 1997.

Riviere, Joan. "Womanliness as a Masquerade." In Victor Burgin, James Donald, and Cora Kaplan, eds., *Formations of Fantasy,* 35–44. London: Routledge, 1986.

Roof, Judith. *A Lure of Knowledge: Lesbian Sexuality and Theory.* New York: Columbia University Press, 1991.

Samuels, Robert. "Art and the Position of the Analyst." In Richard Feldstein, Bruce Fink, and Maire Jaanus, eds., *Reading Seminar XI: Lacan's Four Fundamental Concepts of Psychoanalysis,* 183–86. Albany: SUNY Press, 1995.

Scott, Bonnie Kime. *The Gender of Modernism: A Critical Anthology.* Bloomington: Indiana University Press, 1990.

Sedgwick, Eve Kosofsky. *Epistemology of the Closet.* Berkeley: University of California Press, 1990.

Silverman, Kaja. *The Acoustic Mirror: The Female Voice in Psychoanalysis and Cinema.* Bloomington: Indiana University Press, 1988.

Simmons, Christina. "Companionate Marriage and the Lesbian Threat." *Frontiers* 4:3 (Fall 1979): 54–59.

Sontag, Susan. "Notes on Camp." In *A Susan Sontag Reader,* 105–19. New York: Vintage, 1983.

Stein, Gertrude. *The Autobiography of Alice B. Toklas.* In Catherine R. Stimpson and Harriet Chessman, eds., *Stein: Writings, 1903–1932,* 653–913. New York: Library of America, 1998.

Stimpson, Catharine. "Gertice/Altrude: Stein, Toklas, and the Paradox of the Happy Marriage." In Ruth Perry and Martine Watson Brownley, eds., *Mothering the Mind: Twelve Studies of Writers and Their Silent Partners,* 122–39. New York: Holmes and Meier, 1984.

——. "Gertrude Stein and the Lesbian Lie." In Margo Culley, ed., *American Women's Autobiography: Fea(s)ts of Memory,* 152–65. Madison: University of Wisconsin Press, 1992.

Stopes, Marie Carmichael. *Married Love.* New York: Eugenics Publishing Co., 1931 [1918].

Weeks, Jeffrey. *Sex, Politics, and Society: The Regulation of Sexuality since 1800.* London: Longman, 1989.

Wilde, Oscar. *The Picture of Dorian Gray.* In Merlin Holland, ed., *Collins Complete Works of Oscar Wilde Centenary Edition,* 17–159. New York: HarperCollins, 1999.

——. "The Portrait of Mr. W. H." In Merlin Holland, ed., *Collins Complete Works of Oscar Wilde Centenary Edition,* 302–50. New York: HarperCollins, 1999.

Woolf, Virginia. *The Diary of Virginia Woolf.* Vol. 3. Edited by Anne Olivier Bell. New York: Harcourt, 1980.

———. "Mr. Bennett and Mrs. Brown." In Leonard Woolf, ed., *Collected Essays*, 1:319–37. Toronto: Hogarth Press Ltd., 1966.

———. *Orlando*. New York: Harcourt, 1980 [1928].

———. "Personalities." In Leonard Woolf, ed., *Collected Essays*, 2:273–77. Toronto: Hogarth Press Ltd., 1966.

Zizek, Slavoj. "'I Hear You with My Eyes'; or, The Invisible Master." In Renata Salecl and Slavoj Zizek, eds., *Gaze and Voice as Love Objects*, 90–126. Durham, N.C.: Duke University Press, 1996.

Index

CPSIA information can be obtained
at www.ICGtesting.com
Printed in the USA
BVHW032034220521
607407BV00032B/136